A Ray of Hope

By Allan and Mary

"I Will Restore All the Years the Locust Has Eaten."

Joel 2:25

Published by Connectivity Group LLC
Adamstown, Maryland

A Ray of Hope.
Copyright © 2006 by Connectivity Group LLC.

All rights reserved. No part of this book may be reproduced or transmitted in any form or by any means, electronic or mechanical, including photocopying, recording or by any information storage and retrieval system, without the written permission of the publisher, except for brief quotations in a review.

Published by Connectivity Group LLC on behalf of Allan and Mary, who wish to remain anonymous.

Additional copies of this book may be ordered by contacting Connectivity Group LLC online at *www.cgllcmedia.com* or by phone, fax or mail. Please include your name and contact information in any correspondence. Correspondence directed to the original authors may also be sent to the address below.

Connectivity Group LLC
5950 Norwood Place East
Adamstown, MD 21710
(301) 874-3492
(301) 874-3493 (fax)

The Cover Picture was taken by Allan and Mary while on a pilgrimage to Medjugorje during the healing process, and provided inspiration for the title of this book.

Cover Design by Slice   *www.slice-works.com*

ISBN 0-9789032-0-X

Printed and bound in the United States of America

Dedication

This story is shared to encourage those
suffering from sexual abuse and caught in the mire
of addiction and shame.
Our world is desperately in need
of hope and forgiveness today.

All names have been changed
to protect the identity of those involved.

Preface

This is the true story of how God's grace brought healing and wholeness to one family in a desperate, seemingly impossible situation. Relived through the perspective of both spouses, it documents the pain and agony caused by the disease of sexual addiction where forgiveness and faithfulness are tested to the limit. Who would ever believe that a family could survive all the pain and shame, let alone, become stronger and closer than ever before!

Childhood

Allan

I was born prematurely, weighing just three pounds, and was kept in an incubator for six months while being fed intravenously. I needed to have an operation after an infection developed from the feeding tubes. The scars on my back from that operation grew larger as I grew up and are still evident today. In the 1940's premature babies my size rarely lived. I feel fortunate that I survived.

Most of my young life was spent in and out of hospitals. When I was three, my mother developed severe tuberculosis and was hospitalized for two years. I also tested positive and was confined to a hospital sanitarium for a year until I was free of the disease. Later I was hospitalized for two operations on my severely crossed eyes, and I wore patches as part of the treatment. My crossed eyes improved with glasses but still wandered when I was tired.

My Scottish father worked as a shipbuilder. I have no memory of him, as he died when I was four months old. I grew up knowing him only through my mother's stories and the photographs she saved. Father was a hard worker and very strict.

Growing up I really missed not having a father like other kids. As I matured, I asked more questions about my father. My relatives only shared good things about him, as if there was an unwritten rule not to say anything bad about a family member.

It was a real shock when I read my father's death certificate and discovered he died from cirrhosis of the liver. No one ever mentioned he was a heavy drinker. After this discovery, I asked my Aunt Maggie about his drinking. She became agitated (that unwritten rule again) and immediately changed the subject.

My Irish mother never remarried after my father's death and worked as a registered nurse until she contracted TB. She was a fun-loving, kind, and generous woman—strong in her Catholic faith. She and I spent a lot of time together visiting elderly relatives or friends who were lonely or sick, and she planted the seed of compassion in me.

My first major childhood recollection is starting school. I felt scared and cried because I didn't have a lot of friends. I found school difficult because I was a slow learner. I was awkward, cross-eyed, and scrawny looking with large protruding ears. Kids laughed at me and teased me, calling me names like "elephant ears," "four eyes," and "stupid." I felt embarrassed and ashamed. The teasing hurt and I started thinking, "I'm not good enough. There must be something the matter with me."

My older brother and I fought as kids. I teased him even though he was ten years older and much stronger. I ran fast and usually escaped before he could beat me up. I felt alienated from him because we had little in common. He was stuck with me and endured my presence only out of necessity. By the time I was ten, my brother was off to the Navy, so in many ways, I felt like an only child.

Mary

I was the oldest of twelve children and grew up in a loving, yet chaotic, atmosphere. My father was the youngest in a strong Lutheran farm family and became Catholic when he married my mom. He was a quiet engineer who didn't engage in unnecessary conversation. When he raised his voice to discipline us kids, we knew we were in big trouble. He provided a quiet, loving presence in my life and was always there for me.

My mother was also the youngest child in her family. She did most of the disciplining when I was growing up and was more outspoken than Dad. She was a devout Catholic. Her faith was strong, and she was always reaching out to people in need. Mom introduced me to the lives of the saints when I was young. I loved reading about their courageous adventures and dreamed of becoming a missionary someday.

I drew my own conclusions on what holiness was from the books I read. I thought saints and holy people didn't have negative emotions—they simply accepted both good and bad without ever becoming angry. So I tried to imitate them by being passive, and I became very good at denying my own feelings.

I liked school and did well academically. I was slightly overweight and didn't participate in school sports, preferring to read a good book instead. Inactivity became more ingrained when I broke my leg in sixth grade. The doctor said my growth lines were almost closed, so I probably would not grow much taller than the 4'10" I had already attained. I started my first diet at that time, and began the yo-yo syndrome of dieting and gaining weight that has plagued me most of my life.

Just five months before my eighth grade graduation we moved six hundred miles away. It was a difficult move for my mother and me. We both left behind all our friends and extended family. I was not graduating with the friends I knew since first grade. Worst of all, I hated my new school. I was thrown into a classroom with fifty-six other kids and one elderly nun who had no control of the class. It was chaos, and I didn't handle it well. Often, Mom and I cried together.

Because I was the oldest, I was expected to help take care of my brothers and sisters. I became super responsible, taking on more than I needed to at times. I could get pretty bossy when my siblings didn't do what I expected of them. Looking back I can see that I tended to express my love for others by *doing* things for them rather than just *being*. I measured my own self-worth by what I did or achieved, not by who I was.

Teenage Years

Allan

During childhood, I played doctor and compared body parts with girls and boys in the neighborhood. When I started puberty, I looked at muscle building magazines at the corner grocery store. I longed for a strong body with muscles like the men in the pictures. Instead, I was a skinny ninety-pound weakling who dreaded having to undress and take showers in gym class. I was already feeling embarrassed, awkward, and uncomfortable with my own body when my mother explained that I had an undescended testicle. Now I felt even more different and out of place, and my low self-esteem intensified.

During middle school, some friends introduced me to pornography and masturbation. They looked at *Playboy* magazines and then masturbated. I felt ashamed and dirty watching them. However, the idea of masturbation was planted in my head, and I was haunted by the pleasure they experienced. The world and my so-called friends told me one thing, my church and conscience another.

One time after seeing a movie with friends, one of the kids showed me a shortcut through the woods. He made me drop my pants and pushed me down on the ground and lay on top of me. I was scared. I pushed him off, got up, and ran home. I never told anyone. I felt embarrassed, ashamed, and emotionally drained. I didn't want friends like this, and I became distrustful of anyone who tried to get close to me. Yet I longed to have someone to confide in. My father was dead and my brother was gone. I didn't have a close friend and I couldn't talk to my mother about these things.

I wasn't interested in girls until high school. I was more focused on sports like archery and tennis, and only went to dances because it was the thing to do. My first date was with a friend of the family who asked me to her junior prom. She was the first girl I ever kissed, and I was uncomfortable when she wanted to be more physical.

When I was sixteen, I moved with my mom to Washington, D.C. We lived in an apartment on the grounds of an old estate which had been transformed into a residence for priests doing research and writing books. My mom cooked and I helped clean and garden for the priests. I felt sad and lonely leaving family and friends. I wouldn't graduate with my old class, and going to a private Catholic high school scared me. I was nervous about making new friends, and I didn't know if I could trust anyone. The people in that area were high society and very wealthy. I certainly didn't fit into either of those categories. I felt intimidated and out of my league, like I was from the wrong side of the tracks. I was forced to buy suits and ties to wear to school. I felt pressure from all sides. When I didn't fit into any of the cliques in the new school, my feelings of low self-esteem moved right along with me.

I was an altar server for the priests at the estate. One of the priests, Fr. Walker, who was in his sixties, took an interest in me. We went sightseeing together, visiting museums, historic landmarks, and places of national interest. I loved history, and was fascinated by his knowledge of North and South American history. He became a father figure and I trusted and confided in him. We did a lot of things together, so when he invited me swimming at the nearby pool, I didn't think anything of it. However, in the locker room, I noticed his eyes staring at my private parts. Immediately, the feelings of not being quite normal or measuring up came rushing back to me. I felt very uncomfortable but didn't say anything.

Gradually, Father's advances toward me became bolder until he regularly put his hands down my pants and fondled me. His eyes glistened and he smiled as he touched me. After each abuse there was silence, and then he would send me home. I felt like old garbage being thrown away. I felt angry and confused. I didn't know how to handle the situation. I knew it was wrong, but I felt too scared and ashamed to tell anyone. Priests were held in such high regard that I was sure no one would believe me even if I did tell them. Somehow, it must be my fault. Maybe I was gay and that was why he was attracted to me. I thought there was nothing I could do but endure the abuse. In terms of time, it seemed to go on forever, but in reality it lasted two years. It was during this time that I met Mary.

Mary

I attended an all girls' Catholic high school and was active in the Catholic Student Mission Crusade. I dreamed of being a missionary and planned to enter the convent after high school. I was also involved in the Catholic Youth Organization and became the vice-president of the Washington, D.C. area during my junior year.

I met Allan during a CYO (Catholic Youth Organization) event. He had recently moved from New England, and his accent was so strong I could barely understand him! I made a real effort to reach out to the new kid and introduced him to my brother. We became good friends, and I liked having someone special to hang out with, even though I had no intentions of getting married.

Allan and I had spent a lot of time together, and by the end of my senior year my resolve to enter the convent was weakening. I sought out the advice of Fr. Walker who seemed to have taken a special liking to Allan. He encouraged me to pursue the religious life. I was still torn inside because I liked

Allan, but I resolved my interior conflict by shutting Allan out of my life and pursuing my original goal of becoming a nun. That behavior was typical of my tendency to put goals ahead of relationships and to ignore my feelings.

Relationships

Allan

During my senior year of high school, I met a beautiful girl named Mary. We both belonged to our church youth group and attended the functions. Mary was kind to me. She just wanted to be friends. I was attracted to her because of her beautiful eyes and smile. She was outgoing, and I felt comfortable around her. We soon became friends and spent a lot of time together. I was like another kid in Mary's family. One of her brothers was only two years younger than I, and we camped and hung out together. It was neat being included in Mary's large family. I felt cheated not having any siblings near my age.

My heart pumped faster when I was with Mary and I envisioned spending the rest of my life with her. After we had known each other several months, I asked Mary's parents if I could kiss her. They nodded and smiled in approval, and I gave her a quick peck on the cheek. I was full of joy but careful not to involve sexual feelings. I didn't want our friendship to end because we were becoming too serious, especially after I found out Mary planned to enter the convent. We enjoyed our senior year together. Like normal teenagers, we went to movies, dances, parties, and each other's senior proms.

We talked for hours, but I never told her my deepest secrets. I never mentioned anything about my sexual feelings or the continuing sexual abuse. Mary talked about her desire to be a missionary. She said I would make a great husband and father, but I should also consider religious life. I certainly wasn't interested in that especially with the abuse I was experiencing.

Mary remained firm and chose the convent over me. I hoped she would change her mind, but after we graduated, I went on vacation and she was gone when I returned. She didn't even say goodbye. I felt devastated. I felt rejected and cast aside. I missed the first girl I ever loved and trusted.

After Mary left for the convent, my mom and I moved to an apartment. The sexual abuse stopped, but I had no idea that the emotional scars from this abuse would taint everything I did and eventually consume my life.

Mary

After graduation, I left for the convent and spent the next two years growing spiritually. Our daily routine included morning prayer followed by meditation and Mass. We prayed again in the afternoon and before retiring at night. In addition, our day was filled with chores, college classes, singing, and recreation.

The first fifteen months I loved the quiet atmosphere and felt right at home, but then I started having doubts and felt I wasn't good enough to be a nun. Our wise novice mistress convinced me to stay until I was more certain of God's will.

During our novitiate we learned that marriage was a true vocation that fostered holiness by meeting the demands of a husband and children. I never seriously considered marriage before, and now I needed to find God's will for my life. I prayed and discerned for nine more months. One day as I prayed in the chapel, I was flooded with peace and the certainty that God was calling me to be a wife and mother. When I told the novice mistress of my experience, she agreed with my conclusion. I am very grateful that I remained until I was certain of God's will, and I have never looked back or thought I made the wrong decision.

My mother gave birth to my brother, Dan, while I was in the convent. He was born with Down's syndrome and required extra care. When Dan was ten months old, she became pregnant again, and my mom was very grateful when I returned home. I helped out and slowly adjusted to life outside the convent—that was a real adjustment! I loved the orderly, disciplined life that the convent provided. It was an entirely different world with young children and an endless stream of meals to cook and laundry to wash. I struggled to juggle my need for prayer time with the needs of family life.

When I was not needed at home in the evenings, I started working part-time with Allan. He was friendly but didn't seem interested in resuming our old relationship. I was disappointed but determined to move on with my life. I enrolled in the bachelors program for nursing at a local university. I was naive and sheltered for a twenty-one year old starting college, and I found a safe haven at the Catholic Newman Center on campus.

Allan

After Mary left for the convent, I worked full-time, took college classes, and started participating in a folk dancing group. I met a sophisticated girl named Sharon, who came from a rich upper class family. She went to a well-known private girl's school and a big name college. I wanted to belong to that crowd, but my low self-esteem kept reminding me I wasn't good enough. I was still dating Sharon when Mary came home from the convent. I wasn't ready to resume our old relationship. I was still hurt by the way Mary just left, but I didn't tell her how I felt. When Mary got a part-time job where I worked, I was friendly and talked to her but that was the extent of it.

Sharon and I eventually went our separate ways. I wasn't ready for a permanent commitment, and I felt our family background and expectations were too different. I moved back to New England to be near family and old friends. I continued college classes and found a good job in retailing.

I visited Washington, D.C. the following summer. I was interested in rekindling my relationship with Mary so I asked her to go to the beach. We spent the day together talking about old times. Mary and I picked up right where we left off and I saw her everyday after that until I returned to New England. The spark of our old relationship was still alive. We continued communicating via the telephone and an occasional letter.

It was difficult carrying on a courtship five hundred miles apart and seeing each other only a couple times a year. Eventually Mary moved to New England to be near me. It was wonderful but difficult because my mother wasn't prepared to share me with another woman. There was tension between the two of them until Aunt Maggie intervened and helped my mom to let go.

In addition, two of my friends, whom I had known since childhood, resented the time I spent with Mary. Before I moved away, I went fishing, bowling, and swimming with them, and after I returned, we started hanging out again. The wife of one of these friends wanted to control my life along with her husband's. Mary's presence changed all this and I was forced to choose between Mary and my friends. I am grateful I picked Mary.

Mary

Allan came back into the picture at the end of my first year of nursing school. He was on vacation and visiting friends after moving back to New England. He visited my family and asked my mom if she thought I would still go out with him. She encouraged Allan to ask me, and I was very excited when he did. Secretly, I hoped that we could resume our old relationship. I had seen how Allan treated his mother and others with such great kindness and consideration. I thought he would make a good husband and father; and since I was looking to get married now, I was interested. We spent the day at the beach with another couple and had a great time together.

I enjoyed being with Allan. He was a lot of fun and I felt comfortable with him. We saw each other almost every day for two weeks before Allan returned home.

I went to visit Allan that Christmas. That's when he said, "I was really crushed when you didn't even say goodbye before you left for the convent."

Wow, I didn't even realize he liked me that much!

The following summer when Allan came to visit, we talked about getting married. Allan formally proposed the next Christmas and gave me a beautiful diamond ring. It was difficult being engaged while living so far apart. Allan had a good job as a coordinator for a department store chain and traveled a three state region. He worked hard to be successful. His letters were a great travelogue of all the places he went. He could have published most of them in *Business Week*! Once in a while he called, but I rarely heard words like, "I miss you, honey" or "I can't live without you." From my perspective our courtship was anything but satisfying. I accepted this rather sterile level of intimacy because I was conditioned to ignore my own deep feelings and needs—I was pursuing a goal, which in this case was marriage.

I dropped out of school for financial reasons. I didn't want to go heavily into debt since I had no intention of working as a nurse the rest of my life. I got a good job in the physics department at the university. I worked with a guy named Jerry who had his master's degree in physics. Jerry was single with a lot of worldly experience. We worked closely together and sometimes went to a concert or other cultural event as friends and I enjoyed the attention Jerry gave me. I was already engaged to Allan and it was Allan who possessed the qualities I wanted in a husband, so why was I becoming emotionally entangled with another man? I struggled with the answer to this and was so frightened that I quit my job. It was an extremely difficult decision but I thought by moving closer to Allan the romantic part of our relationship would have a chance to develop.

It wasn't an easy move. I stayed with the grandmother of one of my friends for the first couple of weeks. Allan's mother and I didn't hit it off very well. I think she saw me as a thief who wanted to take away her son. Allan lived at home when he wasn't on the road, and I am sure his mother dreaded the day he would leave. Fortunately, Allan's Aunt Maggie smoothed things over for me, and together they helped me find a small apartment. I obtained another research job and began a new phase of my life.

A few weeks after my arrival, Allan's driver's license was suspended as a result of a speeding ticket he had gotten two months earlier. He was rushing home from an out-of-town trip after receiving word that his mother was very ill. Allan's new 429-horsepower Thunderbird had no trouble going over 100 mph. The only other car on the highway was an unmarked police cruiser. I agreed to drive Allan around while his driver's license was revoked so he wouldn't lose his job. Some of his stores were an hour and a half away, so that meant getting up at five in the morning, picking up Allan, driving him to the store, and then turning around and driving myself to work. After work, I reversed the whole operation. When I finally reached home, I was so exhausted I dropped into bed. This ordeal lasted a month before Allan could drive again.

Allan and I set a date for our wedding and began saving the money to pay for it. During the next eleven months we grew closer but the passionate romance that I hoped for didn't develop. I rationalized that Allan was saving all his affection for marriage. I didn't think a good, long kiss would be out of line since we were engaged. My father always gave my mom a very tender, long kiss every morning before he left for work and that was the expectation I brought to Allan's and my relationship. Unfortunately, that was not to be for me. When I shared that I wanted more than a peck on the cheek, Allan tried for a day or two but any change was only temporary. I wasn't one to rock the boat, so I just accepted the status quo.

Honeymoon

Allan

Mary moved to be near me! She found a job and an apartment. We set a wedding date and began planning. I felt nervous and excited all at the same time. I had never made a long-term commitment before but Mary was everything I hoped for.

By the time we were married, I was ready to settle down. I felt my prayers and dreams were answered. I was marrying my true love and had great expectations. I dreamed of sharing our love together, having children, and owning a home of our own.

Still the remembrance of the abuse haunted me. Surely, if Mary knew my deepest, darkest secret, I would lose her. Keeping this secret consumed my thoughts and affected my ability to be intimate with Mary. The fear of not knowing if I could perform sexually caused me to freeze up and act strange and distant. I was so fearful that I wouldn't measure up to Mary's expectations.

My fears became reality. The first part of my dream was shattered on our honeymoon when I was unable to consummate our marriage. I felt devastated and frightened inside. Mary tried hard not to show her deep disappointment. I couldn't even talk to her about it. Our ability to communicate honestly was breaking down already.

I acted as if this were a minor setback and filled the rest of our honeymoon with sightseeing and other activities. Inside, I was frustrated and angry. The more I tried, the worse things got. I was scared. Was I only half a man? Had the effects of sexual abuse taken a far greater toll than I ever imagined? I didn't know the answer but I wasn't willing to talk to Mary about it. She assumed it was a physical problem and after a year and a half, she finally persuaded me to have surgery to bring down my undescended testicle. The doctor didn't promise the operation would make a difference, but physically and psychologically it enabled me to complete the marriage act.

Mary

We were finally married and all of my preconceived ideas of a honeymoon and marital bliss were shattered right from the start. Allan didn't even seem interested in sex the first night of our honeymoon. I didn't say anything even though I was extremely disappointed. I pushed for intimacy the next night and to my horror nothing worked right. It was difficult to talk about our sexual relationship. I wasn't able to put my feelings into words, and Allan didn't seem comfortable and balked whenever I brought up the subject so I just let it go. We spent the week in Bermuda, touring the island, and hanging out with another couple. I felt deeply disappointed but I didn't tell Allan. I just stuffed my feelings and ignored my deep emotional needs.

Things didn't get any better until I persuaded Allan to go to the urologist. The doctor wasn't sure surgery on his undescended testicle would help, but Allan went ahead anyway. After the surgery we were able to finally consummate our marriage but it was still a struggle. When we went back to the doctor, he gave Allan some strong B vitamins and I was finally able to get pregnant.

Our sex life was still pretty skimpy. I didn't want to ask, and Allan didn't seem all that interested. I felt that my weight or something else must be unattractive to him. Even when I slimmed down it didn't seem to make a difference to him. I convinced Allan to go on a Marriage Encounter weekend with me, hoping that we could talk. It was a great weekend but whenever the subject of sex came up, Allan clammed up or gave vague, noncommittal answers. I was more saddened.

Early Marriage

Allan

We wanted a family, so the doctor gave me medicine to increase my sperm count. Mary finally conceived and bore our first child, a boy whom we named Timmy. I was so proud. Holding my own son filled me with overwhelming joy. I felt like I was going to burst and explode—like fireworks on the Fourth of July. I always dreamed of being a father and I loved it!

We wanted more children and after three years of Mary not conceiving, I started taking the medicine again. This gave me hope that the problem was medical rather than me. It took a year before Michael was conceived but after that we didn't need the medicine anymore. Our son, Paul, was born just sixteen months after Michael's birth.

During this time, I was forced out of a position that I loved to make room for an executive's friend. I was given a new assignment where I was constantly criticized and prevented from doing my job. I was angry, and the old tapes that I wasn't good enough played over and over again in my head. In desperation, I finally gave the company two weeks notice and resigned without having another job lined up.

I turned to a headhunter and started interviewing with different companies. A chain in the Midwest offered me a good job, and Mary and I decided I should accept it.

At the time, Mary was pregnant with Paul, Michael was a year old, and Timmy was four. I should have been on top of the world. My dreams of having a beautiful family and owning my own home came true but the dark cloud that had hung over me since I was abused was now closing in on me. It haunted me—it was always with me. It influenced everything I did, and the fact that I was keeping it a secret, drew me deeper into shame.

The stress I experienced at my previous job, the move, and increasing family responsibilities triggered an attraction to teenage boys that I didn't understand. When I saw them at swimming pools and beaches, I stared at them. Their bare chests brought back memories of my own abuse. I was confused. I didn't understand why I felt this way, and I fantasized about my own physique. In my mind, I was still a ninety-pound weakling coveting muscles and strength. I so desperately wanted to be strong to destroy and overcome the weak and powerless feelings that always weighed me down.

Mary

Allan was treated in a demeaning manner at his job and was so miserable and frustrated that he finally resigned. I was pregnant with Paul and felt insecure without a source of income. After eight weeks of job-hunting, Allan was offered a job fifteen hundred miles away. Within three weeks, we packed up and moved. It was hard leaving family and friends. To make matters worse, the day after we arrived, our son Michael stopped breathing and was rushed to the hospital. He suffered from fever seizures and remained hospitalized for a week. We didn't know anyone and relied on the nurses to find a baby sitter for Tim while I visited Michael. It was a difficult time and I really missed the support of our families.

Our move did nothing to change the lack of intimacy in our marriage. Allan was busy with his job and my time was consumed keeping up with three active boys. I loved the boys deeply but I always wanted a little girl. When Paul was two, I had a miscarriage which was emotionally difficult. Two years later, our only daughter, Marie, was born. I should have been content. I finally had a beautiful daughter and my dreams of a husband and family were a reality, but the emptiness in our marriage gnawed at me. Again I accepted the status quo and stuffed my feelings by keeping busy. I knew things were not the way they should be. I still dreamed of Allan becoming romantic and passionate but it never happened. I never imagined—and was totally unprepared for—the reason behind our lack of intimacy.

Arrested

Allan

My new job went well for several years until the company was sold to the employees. Business was slowing down and politics created a dog-eat-dog atmosphere which became progressively worse over the next five years. Upper management made my job impossible to perform and once again, I was under major stress. I was unaware of plans to sell the company and split up the profits. The managers wanted the company to look profitable and forced higher paid older personnel to resign. I was coerced into leaving along with a lot of other employees.

My mother had died two years earlier and during these times of stress I missed her terribly. I didn't share my feelings of grief with anyone. I felt so horribly alone. Mary was so busy taking care of the kids that it was easy to continue my pattern of not sharing my inner turmoil with her. I didn't share myself physically with Mary very often either. When I did, it was usually in response to pressure from her. The distance between us increased and I retreated deeper and deeper into a black hole.

I started to wrestle with teenage boys in fun. I enjoyed the physical contact and anticipating these encounters gave me a high and helped reduce the stress I was under. I used the wrestling as an opportunity to have inappropriate contact with the boys through their clothes. Eventually these encounters consumed my thoughts and I crossed the line and touched the boys in the same way I was fondled as a teenager. It was like pressing a button inside me and I mentally reverted back to the times when Father touched me, and I relived my own abuse. Deep inside I knew that touching the boys was wrong but the triggers were so strong and overpowering that I couldn't stop. I was so addicted that I didn't even think of my actions as sexual abuse. I fooled myself into thinking we were just playing around and having fun, but I felt so guilty, ashamed, and disgusted afterwards that I always resolved to quit. Then I would get stressed and find myself doing it again.

I was living two lives. On the outside I appeared kind and happy while on the inside I was scared, sneaky, and miserable. Touching the boys was a futile attempt to medicate the pain inside me, which only worsened as I gradually realized I was addicted. I felt worthless and forsaken. I was all alone.

The cycle of abuse continued until the mother of two of the boys confronted me one evening. I was tired of living a double life so when she asked, "Did you touch my boy's private parts?" I answered, "Yes." She screamed, "How could you? You must be sick!"

The reality and seriousness of what I had done came crashing over me. I came home scared and sick inside. I feared what was going to happen to me. The mother of the two boys delayed notifying the police so that I could tell Mary first. I remember sitting on the bed explaining to Mary what I had done. I told her that I also abused the boys from another family in the neighborhood. She was devastated, angry, and shocked. She couldn't believe I had done such a thing. I felt overwhelmed with shame and guilt but relieved that it was out in the open. I still didn't tell Mary about my own abuse. It would be another four years before I could share my deepest secret.

The police came that night and arrested me. Fortunately, my own children were already asleep. The handcuffs around my wrists were so tight they dug into my skin and caused sharp bolts of pain up my arms. The officers threw me into the back seat of a police car and took me to jail where I was booked. I was a criminal now—an outcast. I felt like I had leprosy. I could feel the scorn of the officers as I went through the booking process. Mine was the worst of crimes, the dirtiest. Murderers were held in higher esteem than child molesters. My heart beat fast and sweat rolled down my body. My stomach was tied in knots and my neck felt stiff. The reality and seriousness of my crime consumed me.

I was forced into a damp, dark, cold jail cell. I was exhausted. The fear of going to prison for a long time terrified me. I wanted to die. I felt like my life was over. I tried to sleep on the cold metal bed but I just laid there wide awake and started to think about Jesus. I thought of Him as my friend, someone I could talk to. I was reminded of the faith I learned as a boy and I thought of Jesus' agony and crucifixion. I could see myself at the foot of the cross watching Him suffer for all my sins. I started crying. First one tear rolled down my face and then a stream of tears. The dam of emotions I had stuffed away for years broke loose and I cried my heart out. A guard brought me a sandwich and a blanket. Finally I fell asleep.

I awoke suddenly to a picture of myself with handcuffs and chains sitting in a cell. I took this as a sign that I would go to prison and have to suffer a long time for what I had done. I dozed off again and awoke to the slamming of cell doors and the yelling of drunken prisoners. This wasn't a dream. I was really in jail, separated from Mary and my family. One of the prisoners threatened me, saying, "I will kill you when you come back." I was scared for my life.

The next day Mary posted bail and I returned home. There wasn't a lot of publicity about child molesters back then. The article in the paper about my arrest was an inch long and appeared on a back page. We were spared the media coverage and harassment that is so common today. I felt ashamed and embarrassed seeing my name in the paper. I was now labeled a child molester, pervert, misfit. Understandably, people didn't want to associate with me or my family. They were afraid of me and I felt ostracized. I had to avoid all contact with boys for fear of being accused of further sexual abuse. I also had to be careful about being alone with my own children for fear people would think I was abusing them.

I visited the other family involved, talked with them, and offered to pay for counseling. They were hurt by what had happened but did not want to press charges. The damage, hurt, pain, and anger I had caused the victims and their families was tremendous. I couldn't face having a trial and putting the victims through the agony of describing in public how I had touched them sexually, so I decided that I had to plead guilty and accept whatever happened.

Mary

My whole world was suddenly turned upside down. I was about to hit the wall and lose the life I had taken for granted. As I stirred chili on the stove, Allan came in the front door and asked if we could talk. This was unusual for him. We went to our bedroom and I sat down on the bed and listened. He said, "The neighbor across the street is calling the police because I touched her boys inappropriately."

I looked at Allan. I couldn't quite comprehend what he was telling me. Was he saying he abused the boys? My stomach turned sour. I couldn't believe what I was hearing. Then Allan said, "I also abused two other neighborhood boys." I asked, "Who?" I felt like a ton of bricks dropped on me when he told me it was the sons of a friend of mine.

I was sick inside. Everything drained out of me. I was in a state of shock. It was like watching a horror movie and having to realize it was real. How could he do such a thing? At 10:00, when the police came, the truth of his words hit me. Fortunately, our four children were already in bed, oblivious to what was happening. The police handcuffed Allan, took him out to the cruiser, and left within a few minutes.

Now I was alone with the reality of the situation. I wanted to die. In a very real sense the Mary I had been up to that point did die. I called my mom, who was my support and confidant, and she was as shocked as I was. She wished Allan had been killed in an accident or something rather than this. I had to agree. I hated what Allan had done. It was such a heinous crime. I saw people who did such things as monsters instead of sick human beings. To be married to such a person forced me to take on the worst stigma I could imagine. Death by torture would be easier than to carry such shame. How could I ever forgive Allan or love him again?

I went to bed that night, unable to sleep or make any sense out of what was happening. I could only pray for strength to survive. After a sleepless night, I got up, dropped the children off at school, and went to church. I needed to think and pray. I had to let go of all my dreams and expectations. I had to accept the present reality and begin putting the pieces back together.

I immediately felt compelled to tell my friend that Allan had abused her boys. Would she become angry and never speak to me again? Would she call the police? No matter what—I had to tell her. Words cannot describe how I felt walking up to her front door. I was nauseated and trembling. I was already taking on the shame for Allan's actions. When I told her, she was numb and in total disbelief at first. Then as we talked, she expressed her great sorrow. She and her husband had tried so hard to keep their children safe from the corruption of the world. They didn't even have a television and now this, right in their own back yard! She was not going to file additional charges. She assured me they would work through the abuse with the boys and God would take care of them.

I went home overcome with emotion. What if my children had been abused? How would I react? I felt like divorcing myself from Allan and the whole situation. I was alone in the house, and I prayed and begged God for help. As I agonized, I became increasingly aware that God wanted me to remain faithful to Allan.

On top of all my emotional grief, I had to deal with the legal system. I had no experience with it and didn't know where to start. I called Bob, the leader of our small prayer community. I trusted Bob and looked up to him. His deep faith and prayer life, along with his sound advice, would help me in the days to come. Bob's father was a judge so I knew Bob would know what to do next. Bob called and found out the amount of Allan's bail.

He said, "The first thing you should do is scrape together enough money to post bail."

I was able to come up with the $1,000 and Bob went with me to post bail. Allan and I were actually home before our children returned from school.

In my eyes Allan had committed a horrendous sin. I wasn't sure I could forgive him but I knew God would forgive him if Allan was really sorry. Being Catholic, I desperately wanted Allan to go to the sacrament of Reconciliation. We called a priest friend, Fr. John, and arranged for him to meet with Allan. Father heard Allan's confession and gave him the name of a lawyer and a counselor.

The lawyer wanted to fight the charges and find a technicality that would keep Allan from being sentenced, but Allan insisted on pleading guilty and sparing everyone involved the pain of a trial. In the end the lawyer respected our wishes and tried to do what was best.

We saw the counselor that week. Allan continued seeing the counselor regularly for the next seven months. He also underwent psychological evaluation during that time. The counselor maintained that Allan had missed a stage of development as a teenager and said that in five years this would all be behind us. I was not given the true picture either because of the counselor's ignorance on the subject or possibly his concern that I could not handle the truth at that time. Either way, this assessment left me totally unprepared for what I would face in the future.

It was hard not to believe that I had somehow failed as a wife. I couldn't come up with an obvious reason why Allan had done this horrible thing. I asked him over and over again if he had been abused. Each time he said no. Now looking back on the first sixteen years of our marriage, I couldn't understand how I was so oblivious to what was going on. Allan's refusal to talk about sex and our initial inability to consummate our marriage should have warned me that something was wrong. Why didn't I insist that we get counseling then? Plus there were other, not-so-obvious signs, such as Allan seeming to enjoy the company of teenage boys. I remembered going to bed alone after we had been out for a nice evening together. Allan would stay downstairs watching television or talking with the neighbor boy who sometimes babysat for us. Even though I didn't like his behavior, it was incomprehensible to suspect that anything like sexual abuse was going on.

After Allan's arrest I was very angry. I felt engulfed by darkness and a heavy weight which I couldn't remove. It totally consumed me. I didn't know this person I had married. I felt betrayed. He had been living another life that didn't include me. Again I wondered if I should leave him. What about our children—had they been abused? I certainly didn't want to leave him alone with them.

I was faced with telling our children that Daddy was sick and had touched boys inappropriately while playing games with them. It was easier for me to talk with them one-on-one. I gave the children the amount of information that I felt was appropriate to their age. Then I asked if they ever experienced anything like that themselves. At first they didn't believe their dad did it. Maybe the boys across the street were making it up. Maybe it just happened while they wrestled.

Our children experienced a variety of emotions. Tim was in shock at first but then he became angry and hurt. One of the older victims was Tim's friend, so that compounded the devastation Tim felt. Michael and Paul were younger and did not fully understand when I explained why their father was arrested. Our daughter, Marie, wasn't even in kindergarten yet and was too young to understand.

I felt so alone. I prayed for strength. God would not betray me. It wasn't God's fault that Allan had done this horrible thing. Again during my prayer I felt it was God's will that I stay with Allan and work through this. That was a tall order!

Our daily life became a period of waiting. Not only were we waiting on the court system but we were also waiting on another baby. Shortly after Allan's arrest I found out I was pregnant with our fifth child. It seemed like the worst time in the world to be pregnant. I felt scared and alone. The future was looking like one big black hole. The responsibility of another child seemed overwhelming. All I could do was trust in God. Looking back now, I see that God was weaving the tapestry of my life in a way that I didn't understand. Focusing on new life, rather than my present problems, helped me through this time of crisis. This pregnancy and baby proved to be a tremendous blessing.

The pregnancy intensified the emotional ups and downs I experienced living with Allan during the next seven months. I remember pounding on his chest, sobbing, "Why? Why? How could you do such a thing?" I felt like killing him myself. Yet at other times, the two of us enjoyed lunch together or took a walk and just talked. For the first time in our married life, Allan seemed to need a wife. He wanted intimacy and displayed the kind of passion I had always wanted. The conflicting emotions I felt inside tore me apart. Instead of feeling sacred and cherished, I felt like a prostitute allowing a man who had victimized others to love me.

Three months prior to his arrest Allan was forced to resign from his job. The company was sold and we received severance pay along with some of the profit from the sale. With the extra money Allan and I decided to take Tim and go on an upcoming pilgrimage to Rome, Fatima, and Medjugorje. We made a large down payment for the trip and applied for Tim's passport a week before Allan's arrest.

After the arrest I lost all hope of going and I figured the money was forfeited, but as the departure date neared, our lawyer suggested we ask the judge for permission to go. Fr. John, who was also making the pilgrimage, assured the judge of Allan's return. Amazingly, the judge allowed Allan to leave the country. I was three months pregnant when we left on our pilgrimage.

No matter where we went or what we did I was consumed with trying to make sense of what had happened. I prayed for guidance and strength during the entire pilgrimage. Rome was grueling. I loved seeing St. Peter's and all the holy places but to do it all in two days was exhausting!

From Rome we went to Yugoslavia. We toured the old town of Dubrovnik and then traveled to Medjugorje, three hours away. Fr. John blessed the baby in my womb during Mass and suggested I stay near the church while everyone else climbed Mt. Krizevac.

I spent the entire afternoon praying for Allan, our family, and the strength to survive this ordeal. I felt a deep sense of peace and assurance that God had heard my prayers and would take care of our family.

Pilgrimage

Allan

My lawyer, family, and Fr. John were with me when I asked permission to leave the country. Mary, Tim, and I had signed up for a pilgrimage before my arrest. I was skeptical that the judge would let me go but the lawyer convinced us to at least try. Since I hadn't been convicted or sentenced yet the judge approved the request. It was an absolute miracle that I could go. I felt happy and overwhelmed all at the same time. The trip would offer a respite from the stress we were under and a chance to grow spiritually.

Our son Tim was affected the most by my arrest because he understood the charges against me. I hoped this pilgrimage would give him the strength he needed.

I lived this trip as if it were my last days. One of the customs in Fatima is for pilgrims to walk on their knees on a stone sidewalk about the length of a football stadium. This was done in atonement for sins. I eagerly embarked on this "walk." With every forward movement, I imagined the pain, hurt, and agony I caused others by my actions.

During this trip my emotions fluctuated wildly—low one minute and high the next. I felt excited visiting the holy shrines and churches but depressed from carrying so much emotional baggage. I remember being angry at myself and Fr. Walker, and the prospect of going to prison scared me. I felt alone. Mary was dealing with her own anger and she didn't want to be involved in my pain. Feeling all these emotions helped prepare me for what was ahead.

An experience in Medjugorje greatly strengthened my faith. As we climbed the mountain, Tim and I lost our way. Suddenly we heard bells clanging and a goat appeared with a bell hanging from its collar. We followed the goat and found ourselves on a trail leading up to the cross at the top of the mountain. After a few hours in the hot sun we made it to the top. I felt exhausted, light-headed, and dizzy. Suddenly it started raining and I felt the cool water wash over my whole body from head to toe. A rainbow formed, stretching from the top of the mountain to the church in the valley below. We stood in awe and looked at it for at least half an hour. I had been praying for a sign of God's forgiveness and I knew this was the sign. I felt so grateful and relieved. Through prayer and repentance I made peace with God and myself. I received a gift that day— the strength, courage, and grace I would need to face the future.

When we returned from our climb, a huge crowd was gathered outside the church. We couldn't get back inside to find Mary, so Tim and I waited outside under the dark and cloudy sky. Suddenly the clouds broke apart and the sun started spinning toward us with rays bursting forth like rockets. Then it stopped and started pulsating, withdrawing until the clouds covered it. Sharing this experience brought Tim and me closer and helped to heal some of the pain Tim was experiencing. I truly felt the presence of God. Peace and joy filled my heart. I felt this was a sign that my life would change and things would be different for me now and in the future, but little did I realize the depth and cost of that change.

I returned home to face the psychological testing and evaluation that would influence the judge's decision in sentencing me. Our trip had unforeseen, but understandable, consequences. The mother who pressed charges was angry that I had left the country. She organized a letter writing campaign requesting that I be given the maximum sentence. These letters definitely influenced the judge.

Incarcerated

Allan

Every time that I appeared before the judge I felt emotionally drained. The time between my arrest and sentencing was the longest seven months in my life. I felt like people were staring at me constantly. I was now labeled a child molester, pervert, misfit, and sex addict. The stress of all the psychological tests, weekly counseling, and legal procedures tore me up inside.

Fear of the judge's power over my life—probation or jail—forced me to turn to God for support. I had forfeited control of my life and was at the mercy of God and the courts. Since two of the victims lived across the street, I tried to keep a low profile by not going out of the house unless absolutely necessary. But it wasn't just about me—my family suffered tremendously during this time. They hadn't done anything wrong but they were still looked down upon. The shame of sexual abuse tainted the whole family.

The court procedures and sentencing took a huge emotional toll on everyone—the victims, their families, my family, and me. The mother who pressed charges against me was extremely upset and angry at the length of time the whole process took. I reached the point where I just wanted the sentencing to be over with. I stood firm and would not let the case to go to trial. I was guilty and I didn't want the lawyer trying to prove otherwise.

I got my wish. My day in court finally came. The prosecutor called me a menace to society. He said I should be castrated and locked up for a long time. I stood nervously before the judge, my entire future dangling at the end of a thread. The judge looked at me for a long time and then said, "I sentence you to three years in prison."

I felt devastated, lonely, and ashamed. I wanted to die. In the back of my mind I knew the sentence was fair and justice was being served. The waiting was over. Now everyone could move on with their lives. The healing process could begin for the victims and their families. I apologized to those families and hugged Mary before I was taken away. They stripped off my street clothes, ring, and watch and gave me an orange jumpsuit to wear. I was now a pathetic, frightened prisoner. How far I had fallen!

Mary

I accompanied Allan each time he went to court. I must have loved him, in spite of everything, to put myself through this ongoing ordeal. There was no trial. Allan pleaded guilty but the judge needed the results of psychological testing and evaluation before setting a date for sentencing.

I felt like dying. My legs felt like rubber and could barely support me as I stood before the judge with Allan, waiting for his sentence to be read. The sentence was three years in prison. It was fair. Allan had caused tremendous harm to those boys. I accepted it but I knew it wasn't going to be easy. I dreaded telling our children. How would I deal with their anger on top of my own? How would I meet the physical and emotional demands of four active kids and a newborn baby all by myself?

They handcuffed Allan and took him away immediately. The lawyer then explained that three years actually meant Allan would be eligible for parole in one year.

I came home in the middle of the day to an empty house and the prospect of telling our four children that their father was in prison for at least a year. I was alone in my bedroom and felt numb and overwhelmed. I heard an inner voice clearly say to me, "I will restore all the years the locust has eaten." I didn't know what it meant but I felt a peace that God was with me. (Several months later, I came across this passage in the Bible in Joel 2:25. I didn't remember ever reading it before.)

Each of our children reacted differently when I told them about the sentencing. Tim, the oldest, was very angry and almost put his foot through the dashboard of the car. He was already being ostracized at school. Kids taunted him saying, "Your dad is a child molester." Tim hated what his father had done and didn't want to visit him in prison.

Michael was very sad and fearful. He didn't want his dad going away and felt he was losing him. Paul wouldn't even talk about it. He cried quietly at night and didn't share his thoughts with anyone. Marie was still too young to really understand, but she, too, missed her daddy.

Allan

My memories of incarceration will always be vivid. I can still feel the shackles on my hands and feet and the shame of being stripped naked by the prison staff. Other inmates called me names and even threatened my life. I never experienced anything so humiliating in my whole life. The thought of losing my wife and kids terrified me. Without them there would be no reason to live. I didn't know what Mary planned to do, but I could tell she was struggling with the whole situation. It seemed that being married to a child abuser, in addition to feeling betrayed and lied to, was almost more than she could endure. Would she give up on our marriage and ask for a divorce? I couldn't blame her if she did.

It was hard getting used to the sound of doors clanging as they locked behind me wherever I went in the prison. The barbed wire and guardhouses around the outside of the prison made me feel like an animal in a cage. Living conditions in the prison were severely overcrowded so extra cots were put in the cells. Even the gym was converted into a barracks-style dorm to deal with the increased numbers of inmates. I could see and feel the tension building up within the institution and inside myself. I felt the anger and hatred around me. Everyone was a walking volcano waiting to erupt. Sex and drugs were common. Many of the men in prison were very angry and held bitter grudges. They constantly thought of ways to get back at society for putting them in prison.

Once I saw a prisoner stabbed in the showers. Another time I came outside just as a prisoner was being beaten up by another inmate. I had to be careful what I said and to watch for anyone ready to pounce on me and start a fight. I even worried that another inmate might sexually abuse or kill me. Everything I ever heard about prisons truly happened within these walls.

Prisoners sometimes did cruel things just to amuse themselves. For example, one day as an inmate slept on the grass outside, some prisoners used their cigarettes to start the grass on fire and burn the sleeping prisoner's leg.

Prisoners called me names, spat on me, and tossed food in my face. They threatened me and I learned to trust no one. I saw how people lied and cheated. The system taught shame and kept me living in shame. So I learned how to survive in a tough world. It was survival of the fittest. I saw and learned the mind games people played to stay alive. I found out who was the strongest, the weakest, the most cunning, the most popular, and who was not. I heard many stories about all the different places we could be sent to serve out our time. At times things were so bad I even thought of suicide.

Living in this environment changed my thinking and personality. The caring and thoughtful part of me was being consumed by anger, hatred, bitterness, and fear. I was angry at myself, at God, and at the whole world. But I needed to focus on surviving. I had to make a choice. Did I want to let myself become enslaved by the evil around me or was I going to trust God and accept the suffering that was mine?

After several months in prison I realized how self-centered I had become. Before my arrest I had been a slave to my own passions. I had developed habits of eating, drinking, and spending in excess. I had gone over the edge on all of these and was totally out of control. Now I was brought to my knees. I had reached bottom.

God sent me messengers of faith and love that gave me strength and courage to change my life. The prison ministry visited regularly and a priest came once a month to hear my confession. When I was totally open and didn't try to hide or diminish my sins and failings, I experienced an inner peace that had eluded me for many years. I actually felt freer in prison than when I was enslaved by my secret addiction. I attended a weekly prayer service given by caring Christians from various churches. I signed up for courses and programs on sexual addiction, anger, and empathy for victims. I went to everything that could possibly help me. My time in prison helped me learn about myself. I was beginning to get in touch with my own feelings and the anger I had buried deep inside me when I had been abused. I frequently hit the pillow in my cell just to get the anger out. I found this a healthy way to deal with my feelings of rage and powerlessness.

Visits, letters, cards, and prayers from family and friends kept me going. The love and compassion I experienced gave me hope and enabled me to reach out to other prisoners. I listened patiently as they shared their own stories. I tried to see each one as a person, not a criminal. I shared my food and started making little sacrifices. When an inmate showed interest, I taught him how to pray the Our Father.

One day an inmate told me that Tom, another inmate, was about to commit suicide and needed help. Thoughts raced through my mind—I'm not qualified to handle this but what if I do nothing and he dies? I knew if I didn't do something right away that it would be too late. I understood Tom's feelings because I had felt the same way when I first went to prison. I decided to take the risk and talk to him.

I said, "Tom, God really loves you. He wants to help you. He wants to forgive you, but he won't force you to accept His forgiveness. There is nothing you could do to make God stop loving you."

Tom listened and started sharing about his life and what had led to his imprisonment. He had an alcoholic father who abused him. I shared with Tom that my father was also a heavy drinker and that I had been abused by a priest. We talked, and I was able to give him enough hope to go on living.

The more I reached out, the better I felt about myself. I wanted to make a positive difference in this place filled with so much despair and hate.

Another prisoner was put in my cell with me. My cell was designed for only one person so we were cramped. He was a drug user and picked fights. At the drop of a dime, he would fight over things like someone changing the channel on the TV or just looking at him the wrong way. We were opposites. He was strong and aggressive, while I was weak and passive. We talked a lot because we were cellmates. We shared our stories and eventually became friends. He made sure that nobody hurt me, and I gave him hope and taught him how to pray. I rubbed off on him, and his explosive, self-centeredness gradually changed to thinking of others before acting. He also rubbed off on me in a positive way as I became stronger and more assertive because of his friendship. Even though trust is rarely found in prison, a strong bond of trust and friendship developed between the two of us.

Picking up the Pieces

Mary

When I visited Allan in the county jail, it was a shock seeing him through a glass window in an orange jumpsuit.

Allan said, "I am so scared. Child molesters are the most hated prisoners here."

I told him I could understand that. I felt like the lowest of the low being married to one. Allan was locked up, but I was shackled in my own prison of shame.

Allan asked, "How are the children dealing with everything?"

I explained what a tough time they were having. The parents of some of their friends didn't want them hanging around our kids anymore. Michael came home and told me, "Other kids are making fun of us behind our backs and even to our faces." I told Allan that it is one thing for me to deal with this but I couldn't stand watching the kids go through it too.

After two weeks in the county jail, Allan was moved to the Diagnostic and Evaluation Center where prisoners were evaluated for placement in the prison system. This was an hour away from our home, and I started making weekly trips to visit Allan while the children were in school. Each time I went, the guards thoroughly frisked me. The embarrassment this caused only added to the massive amount of shame I already carried. I felt like the dregs of society and only my faith enabled me to keep facing this humiliation week after week.

Allan's Aunt Maggie was coming from New England to visit us for Thanksgiving. We hadn't told her anything about Allan's arrest in order not to worry her. Now I was faced with dropping this bomb on his poor aunt over the phone. She loved Allan dearly and was like a mother to him. I knew this would be devastating news.

When I told her, like many people from that generation, she just shoved the whole thing under the carpet and proceeded as if nothing happened. She still came for Thanksgiving and even braved going to the prison with me. She demanded, however, that we not tell Allan's brother anything about it. This was possible because his brother lived fifteen hundred miles away, and we only talked to him on holidays and birthdays.

Aunt Maggie suggested the children and I fly to my parents' for Christmas. They lived on a farm with a lake for ice-skating and lots of land for skiing and snowmobiling. It was a great distraction and getaway for the kids and it gave me some much-needed rest. Our visit was emotionally difficult for my mother. She was in anguish over the whole situation with Allan and our presence seemed to intensify her pain. It was hard for us to talk and I felt alienated from her. Thankfully after our initial difficulty, my mom put her own feelings aside and reached out to me in love and support.

When we returned home, I focused on getting ready for our new arrival. In addition to the normal routine of cooking, laundry, and driving kids everywhere, I started cleaning everything and sorting through drawers and closets. This project was a great way for me to escape pain and avoid dealing with my negative feelings, and I was grateful for the distraction.

Andrew finally came. My two best friends went through labor and delivery with me. It was strange not having Allan there. I felt like I was having a baby out of wedlock. I worried, "What kind of future would Andrew have coming into a family with the father in prison?"

My parents came when I got home from the hospital, and I don't think I could have managed without them.

By the time Andrew was born, Allan had been moved to a medium security facility which was less restrictive, so I was able to bring Andrew and a picnic lunch when I went to visit. Allan was overwhelmed with emotion when he saw Andrew for the first time. It made all the more poignant the fact that he missed Andrew's birth and could not participate in his children's lives for at least a year.

Allan talked about his schedule and the treatment programs. I told him the news from home and what the kids were doing. Occasionally, I could get the four older children to go along but not very often. They hated going. They felt traumatized by the security procedures and very ashamed of their father. Tim was haunted by the sound of the heavy doors unlocking and slamming as Allan was moved to the visiting area. He just wanted to cry when he heard them call his father's name and saw Allan appear in an orange jumpsuit. Michael missed his dad. The cold, stark reality of the prison really bothered him. He was very sad and said he did not want to come anymore. Paul became sullen and withdrawn. He had a hard time talking to his father. Marie didn't like the prison at all. Seeing her father together with a lot of other prisoners in one large room scared her.

During Allan's imprisonment, I didn't look at the future. I just focused on day-to-day survival. I completely immersed myself in the life of my children, trying to be both mother and father. Even though I was reticent to talk about my feelings with Allan, I was able to listen and encourage our children to talk openly and honestly about their feelings. We talked about school and the reactions of people who knew what their father had done. Tim described how a kid deliberately poked him in the hand with a lead pencil while calling his father a pervert. Another time a kid laughed in his face as he pushed him to the ground. Michael missed having friends over but said the teachers at school were going out of their way to be extra nice. Marie had just started kindergarten and said she missed her daddy. It really wasn't until each of the kids became teenagers that the deep anger and resentment they felt surfaced.

The children and I received counseling every week for the entire year Allan was in prison. The counselor worked a lot with Tim, who was closest to his dad and felt very alone and isolated because he didn't have any good friends. Michael, on the other hand, was popular and handled the situation much better emotionally. The counselor encouraged Paul and Marie to talk while playing board games.

Counseling helped me deal with the everyday stress of life, but it didn't give me a clear understanding of the addictive nature of Allan's actions. It left a lot of questions unanswered. God had provided for us financially through the sale of Allan's former company, so I made the time after counseling special by taking the children to a restaurant. All the children were involved in gymnastics prior to Allan's arrest, so they continued to participate in local and out-of-town meets while Allan was in prison. This was costly, but well worth it, as it kept them occupied and gave them something to look forward to.

I did a lot of driving as a single parent and didn't always focus on what I was doing. Often I was distracted and made stupid errors like turning left directly in front of an oncoming car. Another time I was going the wrong direction down a one-way street. Once the kids warned me when I was about to hit the car in front of me. Miraculously, we never had an accident.

One of the ways I dealt with my negative feelings about our marriage and sexual relationship was to totally gut our bedroom, the junk room of the house. My sewing machine and an old metal filing cabinet were squeezed into it, and the laundry always ended up on our bed. To top it off, the bedroom set, which I hated, was falling apart. So I took everything out of the bedroom and redid the whole room. I painted the walls and bought new carpeting and a beautiful bedroom set. The final touch was new curtains with a bedspread to match.

Redoing our bedroom gave me a concrete outlet for my feelings of wanting a totally fresh start with Allan when he came home from prison. I wanted all this behind us. I had high hopes that Allan and I would finally be able to establish a close relationship and that he would need me as a wife. I naively expected that he would be healed of whatever had caused him to be abusive.

Toward the end of Allan's first year in prison, I appeared before the parole board which was considering allowing Allan to return home. They recommended that the children and I start seeing a counselor of their choice in preparation for Allan's return. None of us liked this new counselor. She was too blunt and seemed to be rubbing vinegar into the raw wounds of our hearts. She threw cold water on any hopes I had for us being a happy family again. She told us that Allan was likely to abuse again, and male friends of the children should not come into our house.

She compared our situation to having an elephant in the living room. She said we could ignore it and pretend it wasn't there or we could acknowledge its presence and deal with it. Those were hard words to swallow and it took time before I understood and accepted their validity. Soon I would find out for myself just how long and painful the journey to wholeness would be for our family.

Freedom

Allan

After a year in prison, I was released on parole. Leaving prison was a bigger adjustment than I anticipated. Even though I was on the outside, I still felt like a prisoner. I reported weekly to my parole officer who made it clear that he hated child molesters and sex offenders. He always made me wait a long time whenever I came for my appointments. He interrogated me about everything I did and repeated the same questions over and over again. I felt he didn't believe me and was trying to find a way to send me back to prison. I didn't trust him.

One condition for my parole was that I have a full-time job. A friend of ours who was always coming up with new business ventures gave me a job putting together and marketing restroom travel kits. It was during the time of the AIDS scare and he thought they would sell. Unfortunately, they never caught on and at the end of parole I still needed to find a stable job.

The first time I went back to church, I felt fearful and nervous. I imagined what people must be thinking and saying about me. At the handshake of peace, the family behind me smiled, held my hand tightly and said, "Welcome back." Immediately I relaxed and felt welcomed. After Mass, Father said, "Welcome back home, Allan." That gave me a sense of relief and joy in my heart that someone cared about my family and me.

Mary insisted that we renew our wedding vows. For me, it was a commitment to change myself. The words, "I take you, Mary, to be my lawful wedded wife, for better or worse, in sickness and in health until death do us part" meant a lot to me.

It was a new beginning in our lives. I hoped that this time my relationship with Mary and the children would be closer and not haunted by my past mistakes. I was aware of the need to restore Mary's trust in me. We had lived apart for a year, and I was scared of the effects my imprisonment would have on our future.

At Christmas our church brought us a food basket and presents for everyone. I broke down and cried. The gesture humbled me. I found it hard to be on the receiving end. I felt unworthy of so much kindness.

Being locked away in prison for a year had dramatically changed my family and me. We all had major adjustments to undergo when I came out. I feared that everyone was watching me, and I walked around with extreme caution. I faced the difficulty of finding a regular job with a felony on my record. I got sick inside every time I filled out a new application and checked yes when it asked if I had been convicted of a felony. I answered truthfully and I soon realized my job options were limited.

Before my arrest Mary and I had belonged to a small prayer group that met every week. We prayed together, and like a family, we celebrated major events together. This prayer group had been Mary's biggest support during my imprisonment, but when I came home, they told me I could no longer be a part of the group. Everyone had a lot of children and they were not comfortable with me around. I understood, but it still hurt me deeply. These were our closest friends. Mary was welcome to continue without me and this posed a huge dilemma for her. In the end, Mary chose to stay home with me.

As people pulled away and dropped out of our lives, Mary felt lonely and concerned about the possibility of my repeating the abuse. She eventually convinced me to try a new counselor, who introduced me to a twelve-step support group, Sex and Love Addicts Anonymous (SLAA).

I was really scared going to my first meeting. I didn't want people to know why I was there. I feared meeting someone I knew who might tell others about my addiction and actions. After my first meeting, I felt tremendous relief learning that others battled sexual addiction too. This was my first true feeling of relief. Before this I thought I was the only one. It was like having a black cloud over my head. Now, for the first time, I knew I wasn't alone. Five days a week I listened to others share their hurts, pains, and struggles. I started to learn about myself and about the disease of sex addiction. I never knew others felt just like I did.

I chose someone in SLAA who I really admired for a sponsor. Working with him on the twelve steps to recovery made me accountable to someone other than myself. I began reading books on the subject and developed friendships with other members of the group. I found acceptance and did not feel judged. My thinking changed as I discovered I could be honest about my feelings and still be accepted. This was new to me. I had always kept my true feelings and thoughts to myself. For the first time in my life, I found a place where I didn't have to hide my secret. Sharing my own abuse and actions with the group brought me tremendous freedom and relief, but I still didn't dare share any of this with Mary.

Facing Reality

Mary

After a full year, Allan came home from prison. I didn't feel married to him. He certainly wasn't the man I thought I had married and I wasn't sure if I loved him anymore, but in my heart I felt certain God wanted me to remain faithful to Allan. So I requested that we exchange our wedding vows again. I needed a new start.

Like any new marriage, exchanging the vows is only the beginning. Constantly we faced the consequences of what Allan had done. He couldn't get a regular job because of his felony conviction and his lack of confidence.

With Allan home, we could no longer be part of our prayer group because of the children present. My best friend, Andrew's godmother, no longer talked to me because she feared Allan had touched one of her boys. Losing this friend was and still is a great sorrow for me. She was such a wonderful person that the loss of her friendship was especially distressing, and her actions caused me to reevaluate my decision to stay with Allan. Going against the popular opinion and advice of my friends was draining even though I was convinced it was God's will for me.

The counselor was fairly certain that Allan had never abused our own children but I still did not want to leave him alone with them. Our boys couldn't have friends over and this fact brought home the reality of the situation for them. It was so unfair and terribly difficult for them. I was beginning to grasp the addictive nature of Allan's actions. I was uneasy and constantly on guard. My lack of trust in Allan added to the alienation and separation we experienced with each other.

This was the worst of times for our children. Tim was in high school, and although no one at the new school knew about his father, he struggled to make friends. Michael lost respect for his father and was angry at God. He asked, "Why me—why anyone?" Paul was having difficulty in school and disdained Allan's authority. I was forced to do the disciplining even after Allan came home.

My spiritual director recommended that Allan see a counselor who was involved in a program for sex and love addiction. I pushed Allan into giving the program a try because the thought of Allan repeating his abusive behavior terrified me.

After we renewed our wedding vows, our attempts at intimacy were disastrous. The same problems that plagued our first year and a half of marriage returned. Our inability to have normal relations frustrated me and my hopes of something better were shattered. We slipped into a routine of living together as brother and sister. Each of us retreated more deeply into ourselves, trying to make the best of a difficult situation. This continued for the next twelve years.

Allan

I settled for two part-time, minimum wage jobs because of my felony conviction. I felt like a total failure as a father and husband when I was unable to make enough money to provide basic food and shelter for my family. I swallowed my pride and applied for food stamps. The final blow to my ego came when I was let go from one of my jobs and my boss hired Mary because of her technical experience. I stayed home while Mary worked

The stress triggered old tapes in my head to replay, saying, "You're not good enough, you can't do anything right" and the thought of acting out (a term used in SLAA to describe addictive behavior) went through my mind. For now, I resisted the temptation.

The role reversal was emotionally hard because Mary was busy all the time and didn't have much time and energy left for me. She resented going to work and was still angry over all the pain I had caused the family.

I wanted to fix everything but the more I tried the worse it got. I felt overwhelmed by the demands of five children and their different schedules. Chauffeuring kids to four different schools and sports activities kept me on the run. There was always something to do and I couldn't just come home and relax like I did when I worked a regular job. I had little free time because Andrew was still so young and I was learning how to cook and do laundry. As I adjusted to the routine, however, I began to find the time at home healing.

I saw firsthand the emotional impact of my crime and imprisonment on our children. My oldest son, Tim, had difficulty making friends and started hanging out with kids who abused alcohol. At the beginning of his junior year, he was involved in a major car accident and shortly after that was diagnosed with mononucleosis. He fell far behind in his studies and was forced to drop out of school. I felt I was to blame for much of Tim's difficulties. I felt frustrated, hurt, and deeply sorrowful. There was nothing I could do to change things for him.

Tim finally went to live with Mary's parents and enrolled in a new school. Unfortunately, his troubled behavior continued. He skipped school and gave the principal a hard time. Mary's parents were at their wits' end. When they heard about a program for troubled teenagers in Arizona, they immediately arranged for Tim to go. The program gave Tim a new start and after a month he was able to return home.

Tim earned a GED and enrolled in a community college where he took classes for two years. He was carrying a lot of pent-up anger inside. One day he came home and punched me in the face for no apparent reason, and I needed stitches to repair the damage. The punch showed all the anger and hurt he felt towards me.

Michael seemed to be socially secure and self-confident. He appeared happy on the outside but still suffered embarrassment and shame from his peers. One of Michael's teachers intercepted a note at school that read, "WANTED DEAD OR ALIVE" with a hand drawn picture of me underneath.

Paul became withdrawn and was having trouble in school. I worried that he would drop out also. Marie and Andrew were too young at that time to realize the severity of the situation.

It tore me apart to see all the devastation and hurt that our children endured because of my actions. My family was suffering for something they didn't do. I was forced to acknowledge the consequences of my actions, and it was extremely painful—seemingly unbearable at times.

Mary

My world turned upside down again when we received a phone call from Jim, an engineer friend, who had employed Allan part-time. Allan is a people person and not adept at mechanical endeavors. Jim was facing a deadline and needed someone with technical experience. He offered me a full-time job, saying he had to let Allan go. Andrew was only two and a half, and I hadn't worked outside the home for fifteen years. The whole idea was frightening. Allan and I discussed the situation and decided I should take the job. When we called Jim back to tell him of our decision, he said, "Can you start tomorrow morning at seven a.m.?"

My working only added to the stress in our family. Allan became Mr. Mom and I resented giving up my traditional roles. Allan cooked and cleaned while I felt like an outsider in my own kitchen.

Six weeks after starting work, I went back to school. I needed to finish college if I was to support our family. I didn't have time to be involved in the day-to-day happenings at home. I didn't even have time to play with the kids. Deep inside, I resented Allan for not providing for our family.

I allowed my prayer time to slip also. I prayed but it wasn't the heartfelt relationship with a loving God that I was used to. Prayer became just another "should" in my life that I squeezed into my already overcrowded schedule.

Forgiveness

Allan

How could I find peace in my heart? How could I forgive Fr. Walker for ruining my life and the life of my family? The abuse which occurred thirty-seven years earlier still haunted me. I never told Mary my dark secret and even after my arrest, I repeatedly denied being abused.

One evening, I went with two other members of SLAA to talk about the program and share our stories with a group of prisoners who were being released to a halfway house. As I told my story and talked about being sexually abused as a teenager, I noticed prisoners with sad and withdrawn faces looking down at the floor. When I continued and said I had crossed the line and abused others, their faces changed to anger and disgust. I could feel the tension and hate. One of the prisoners just glared at me. If looks could kill, I would be dead. I was scared and wanted to run away.

We explained about SLAA and how it could help them adjust to the real world after being in prison. The prisoners talked among themselves and afterwards one of them came to me and said, "You had a lot of courage to come here and admit what you did. You showed me there is hope even for a sex addict. Thank you."

I came home and sat down next to Mary. She asked how my meeting went.

I said, "I was so scared. The prisoners looked at me with such disgust and hatred when I shared what I had done."

Mary answered, "I'm not surprised. Most of the people in prison have been abused in one way or another." Mary looked me in the eye and said, "Are you sure you were never sexually abused? What you did just doesn't make sense."

I couldn't hide it any longer. I broke down, cried like a baby, and finally told her, "Fr. Walker sexually abused me." I couldn't go into detail, but at least the secret I had so carefully guarded was finally out. With the tears came a tremendous sense of relief. It felt like opening the window, letting fresh air into a room that had been closed off for years.

With the secret out, I was able to move to a new level of forgiveness, both for myself and Fr. Walker. The image of the prodigal son came vividly to mind. I saw how anxiously the father had waited for the son's return. Gradually, I was able to accept the forgiveness God offered me at a deeper level.

I was working on the eighth step which was to make a list of all people we had harmed and become willing to make amends to them all. During this process, my sponsor suggested that I forgive the person who abused me. My first reaction was, "I can't do that." Then I realized that if God had forgiven me, then I had to forgive Fr. Walker—but how? I knew I couldn't do it by myself so I prayed and asked God to help me. It was then that I realized that forgiveness was absolutely necessary for me to heal. God touched my heart, and slowly over time, I was able to forgive Father. Mary suggested I put my thoughts and words into action by writing Fr. Walker a letter.

After I told Mary of my abuse, she wrote an eight-page letter to Fr. Walker pouring out all her feelings and frustrations. She never mailed it and finally tore it up. We decided it would help us let go of the past if I wrote Father an acceptable but informative letter. Father was old and we wanted him to know that we forgave him. With the help of my counselor, I wrote the following letter:

Dear Fr. Walker,

I have experienced a lot of hurt and pain since I met you. I have kept this a secret and thought that by stuffing it away I would forget it. Unfortunately, I didn't and acted out on other people the abuse that had been perpetrated on me. As a result of this behavior, I hurt my family, relatives, and friends.

I spent one year in prison, separated from Mary and my family. I have been receiving counseling for the last five years and am recovering from sex and love addiction. My family has suffered tremendously because of what has happened, and there were very serious consequences for our children, especially our oldest son, Tim. He has suffered great stigma from his peers because of my actions. I am not working at present because it has been difficult to get and hold a job with a felony conviction. Mary has had to go to work to support our family.

I have gone through a lot of hurt, anger, hatred, bitterness, resentment, sorrow, and pain. It has taken me a lot of years to forgive you, but I want to tell you, I do forgive you.

We know that 95% of those who abuse others have been victims themselves. It is probable that you too have been a victim and may have totally blocked it from your consciousness. People who are good and spiritual can still do things that are not life enhancing.

My life has changed for the better even though I must bear the consequences of what I did. I am making healthy choices now and know a freedom and peace I couldn't before.

We are enclosing a research paper that Mary wrote and beg you to read it.

Receiving and giving forgiveness makes us open to God's love, and we hope someday to embrace you in Heaven.

Allan

(See Appendix A for Mary's research paper.)

A couple of weeks later we received a letter back from Father. At first I felt nervous and afraid to open it. He wrote:

Dear Allan,

Yesterday I received your letter, and I can say candidly that yesterday was the saddest, most frustrating, most humiliating day in many, many years. How I wish I could roll back the years and avoid the evil I have done. But in all this grief and sadness, all this pain and tragedy, there was one bright ray: you are a better man than I am, for, despite it all, you wrote, "I want to tell you that I forgive you." For years I have found it exceedingly hard to forgive myself. Your words bring me immense relief, and so does the paper that Mary wrote. There is so much in it that is true of my early life. Now I wish I had even half of that information then, but we had none.

I want you to know that I share with you in all this tragedy, and words of apology from me would be entirely inadequate. I am now very old, and I realize I do not have much time left, but because of God's wonderful mercy, I know He has a place for me in Heaven. When I get there, one of my first requests will be: Dear Lord, take good care of Allan and the family, today and every day. And that prayer will continue until you and I meet in Heaven. There it will be easy to ask and receive forgiveness.

I wish I was well enough to write a longer letter, but I feel that you will understand. Do not bother replying to this. I shall now die more happily for I realize that you have forgiven me.

God bless you and your dear family. May He console you and take care of all of you.

Fr. Walker

I am glad that I had the courage to open his letter. His acknowledgement of what happened helped lift the burden of anger, hurt, and pain which I had carried around for over thirty years. Tears ran down my face, and peace flowed into my heart. The words and message contained in Father's letter helped me on the road to recovery. That day was momentous in my life.

Mary

I threw myself into work and school and tried to deal with the issues at home. Tim, our oldest, developed serious behavioral problems and was failing in school. At various times, all three teenagers were caught drinking. Tim got a DWI, Michael a citation for a minor in possession of alcohol, and Paul totaled a car while drinking. The last thing Paul could remember was driving on the interstate. His car ended up at the bottom of a hill, miles away.

Paul's anger was finally starting to surface. He yelled at me, "Dad is not worthy of my respect. I am repulsed by his presence. I don't trust him around my friends. I despise him."

I was sick and my heart was broken. Our family was falling apart. I was doing everything I could, but it wasn't enough. I couldn't heal all the bitterness and pain our children experienced.

These years after Allan's return from prison strained our marriage almost to the breaking point. I had already experienced so much pain and things were just getting worse. At times, I lashed out at Allan and blamed him for all our problems. I almost gave up. The anger, shame, and bewilderment I felt just grew deeper. I didn't know what to do.

Nothing made sense. I couldn't understand why Allan abused those boys. He constantly denied being abused, and yet everything I read said people who abuse are usually victims themselves. Allan always appeared kind and happy, and I rarely saw him exhibit impatient or hostile behavior. In fact, I was the one who was impatient.

Allan finally shared his own abuse with me several years after his arrest. He went to talk about SLAA to a group of prisoners. When he came home, he seemed shaken and shared with me his terrifying memories from prison and how frightened he was returning. He worried about being attacked when telling his story.

I was getting a rare glimpse into Allan's feelings, so I took advantage of his openness to pursue my suspicions. I coaxed Allan until he choked out, "Fr. Walker abused me." That was all he could say.

Fr. Walker was alive and I knew him. He was still sending us a Christmas card every year. I talked with him before entering the convent, and he witnessed our vows when we married. I suspected abuse in Allan's life, but nothing in my life's experience prepared me to understand what Allan was telling me now. I felt sick inside. This revelation shook me to the core of my being. I loved my Church. My faith kept me going. I felt numb. I could hardly believe what Allan was saying. It was inconceivable to me that a priest could do this. All the pain of the past six years came flooding back. I couldn't let Allan know how upset I was. I went to church the next day when no one else was around, and I just sobbed and sobbed. Kneeling in front of the altar, pounding the steps with my fists, I cried out, "Why God? Why?"

I went to see our pastor, but he didn't understand my pain. He patted me on the head and said, "It's all over with.

Just forget it and move on." I felt like punching him in the nose. How could he so casually dismiss that a priest had done such a thing?

However, he did send me to a wonderful counselor who gave me permission to feel all the negative emotions that were boiling up inside me. I poured out all my anger and hurt over what Allan had done, my deep disappointment in our marriage, and my grief that a priest could sexually abuse. I also started journaling my feelings.

During this time, Allan and I also attended a twelve-step program called *New Life,* designed to help people heal and find peace in God rather than in addictions or codependent relationships. I went through the twelve-week program as a participant twice and a third time as a facilitator. It was a safe place to talk out my feelings and examine my own attitudes and means of coping.

My first week as a facilitator will be forever etched in my memory. There were seven women in our group, and we each introduced ourselves and shared what brought us to *New Life*. As facilitator, I was last and all the women before me shared how they were abused sexually and emotionally during their life. By the time it was my turn, I had taken on all the shame of the entire group! I was married to an abuser and that made me guilty by association. I felt like the lowest of the low. I was carrying the shame for what Allan had done. Only God could heal me and restore our family.

I wrote an emotional eight-page letter to Fr. Walker expressing all my anger and hurt. I never sent that letter but putting those feelings down on paper helped me work through them. I also did extensive research and wrote a paper on sexual abuse of boys for an English class I was taking. The research helped me understand Allan and how the cycle of abuse perpetuates itself, causing so much harm especially when the abuse is kept secret.

I encouraged Allan to write his own letter to Fr. Walker, and I was happy with the letter he finally sent along with a copy of my paper. I felt God kept Fr. Walker alive long enough to receive Allan's letter and write back. He died at the age of ninety-two, shortly after replying to Allan's letter.

I still struggled with anger and unforgiveness both toward Allan and Fr. Walker. In the Our Father, I prayed, "Forgive us our trespasses as we forgive those who trespass against us" but I surely didn't feel like forgiving. All the negative feelings inside me just wouldn't go away. I knew if I wanted God to forgive my sins, I had to forgive Allan and Fr. Walker from my heart, so I made a conscious decision to pray for the grace I so desperately needed.

God would meet me where I was. I didn't have to feel like forgiving. I just had to be willing to ask for the grace. I knew I couldn't do this on my own. I needed God to do for me what I could not do for myself. I found a prayer that encompassed all the areas where I needed forgiveness in my life, such as forgiving myself, my parents, my spouse, in-laws, relatives, neighbors, etc., and I started to pray it every day. (See Appendix B for forgiveness prayer.) I reasoned that if I were faithful in praying and wanting to forgive, even though I didn't feel like it, then God would do something to change me. Just saying the prayer made me more conscious of the peace I was seeking and how much I wanted to stop being angry and how much I wanted to forgive.

This period of my life was a constant struggle to put one foot in front of the other and keep going. I continued to say the forgiveness prayer every day for two years. God finally answered my prayers in a miraculous way. Again I shared my anger and struggle to forgive with my spiritual director. I went to Confession, and when Father placed his hands on my head and prayed the prayer to absolve my sins, time stopped. I was engulfed in love. It was no longer the priest there but Jesus himself.

God's love totally enveloped me. Jesus' hands were on my head, and I felt His love washing over my whole body. I was washed clean. All the anger and shame I felt previously was replaced with love. I thought that this must be what Heaven will be like—total love! I was living between Heaven and Earth. I felt so grateful, and I found it easy to love everyone and make sacrifices for others. This was a true miracle in my life, and I did nothing to be worthy of this grace—I simply asked for the grace to forgive.

The tension in our home diminished after this. We started to laugh again, and I wasn't slashing Allan with the knife of my sharp words. I felt peace inside and began to notice how other people felt. The impossibility of our situation no longer consumed my life.

Status quo

Allan

While Mary worked full-time and attended college, I had no choice but to be home with the kids. I had to be Mr. Mom. After Mary received her bachelor's degree, she spent more time with the family and took back some of her traditional roles. The first thing I handed over was the cooking. I spent a lot of time making a meal that Mary could throw together in minutes.

Tim resented Mary's going to work and was having difficulty coping with life. One day he packed up his belongings and walked out saying, "Don't try to contact me. I don't want anything to do with you."

We didn't realize that Tim was mentally ill and suffering from paranoid schizophrenia. For a whole year we didn't see or hear from him. I felt so helpless, scared, and worried about him. I was afraid we would never see him again. My heart was broken. I thought of myself, growing up without a father—now I couldn't be with my own son.

With Tim gone and Andrew in school during the day, I was ready to find a job and go back to work. I found a part-time telemarketing job but felt intimidated going back into the work force after five years at home. Gradually I gained self-confidence in my ability to do a job.

My relationship with Mary still lacked sexual intimacy. We gave up after our initial attempts when I first came home. Mary never mentioned it, so I just avoided the topic. We both accepted the status quo and settled for a survival mode in our marriage.

When I started working, I continued my SLAA support group but drastically cut down the number of meetings I attended. I didn't make time for phone calls or visits to keep in close contact with people in the program. I started seeing my sponsor monthly rather than once a week. Because I had been in SLAA for nine years, I felt confident that I had turned the corner and all the abuse tendencies and issues were behind me. I felt in control. That confidence proved to be my downfall.

Mary

The summer before Michael's senior year of high school, we had a family reunion. My brother, his wife, and their four young children really liked Michael. They offered him free room and board and a car if he came to live with them while attending college. This seemed like a good idea. It would give Michael a chance to develop an identity of his own away from the stigma of our family. My sister-in-law had worked through abuse issues with her own father and would help Michael through the healing process. Michael finished his senior year and flew to my brother's on the East Coast a week after graduation.

Paul graduated from high school the following year. He no longer drove a car because he couldn't get insurance after five accidents. Paul was changing the direction of his life in a positive way and spent the summer after graduation working with me on our house. It was a time of bonding for us.

Paul inherited his grandfather's technical mind, and we tackled replacing rotted sections of flooring, a door jam, and all the molding that was too damaged to refinish. We repaired and refinished all the cabinets and drawers in the kitchen and bathrooms. Paul sanded during the day, and in the evening and on weekends, we worked together cutting trim and doing the finishing work. At the end of August, our house looked like new, and Paul left for college.

Marie turned sixteen and was involved in relationships with boys. The implications and impact of her father's crime began to eat at her. She found a job at a pizza parlor and stayed there after hours to avoid being around her father. Often I tracked her down at two in the morning to drag her home. In her junior year, the school suggested she get counseling. The counselor included me for part of each session and after two months suggested Allan also attend. Marie didn't like the counseling and only went reluctantly.

Marie was developing a relationship with one of her managers at work, Luke. He was a year ahead of her in school and would soon graduate. Luke accompanied Marie to many of her counseling sessions, and his understanding and support brought Marie through this difficult time.

Paul decided to enter the seminary at the end of his sophomore year in college. He wanted to tell his brother, Tim, and talk to him before he left, but Tim had severed all contact with the family. We didn't know exactly where he lived and hadn't seen him for a year.

We heard rumors that he worked for a local business, so Paul played detective, calling all the apartment complexes in the city. He narrowed his search down to one large complex not too far from our home. Paul went through each of the buildings looking for Tim's name on the mailboxes until he found it. Tim was not home, so Paul made it a practice of driving through the complex whenever he was in the area, hoping to find Tim. His persistence paid off, and one evening he found Tim working under his car so he stopped to talk.

Tim invited Paul into his apartment, and Paul was horrified at what he found. His only furniture was a bed. Cockroaches were everywhere. Tim opened a drawer stuffed full of unpaid bills. Paul convinced Tim to re-establish contact with the family. We gave him some used furniture and asked the management to exterminate the cockroaches. Tim made payments on his bills until he was hospitalized for schizophrenia and forced to file bankruptcy.

Andrew, the youngest, was now eleven. He was a happy child who was loved and spoiled by everyone in the family. He liked to tease his older brothers, and they gave him a good dose of his own medicine. We had settled into a more relaxed and contented atmosphere when WHAM! we were struck again—Allan had a relapse.

Relapse

Allan

After ten years in SLAA, I relapsed and slipped into my past behavior. I had been in the program a long time and felt smug and confident. I thought I was in control. I fooled myself into thinking I was healed after so many years without a relapse. At the time, I attended only one SLAA meeting a week and was too busy to actively work the twelve steps. I didn't pay attention to my red flags either, such as staring at teenage boys for a long time, spending time alone with them, or thinking of ways to gain their trust.

These were warning signals of my sexual addiction, and I ignored them. I allowed myself to spend time with Jack, a friend of Marie's who occasionally came to visit. I spent more and more time visiting with him—ten minutes, fifteen minutes, half an hour. This should have been a signal for me to stop and re-evaluate the situation but I chose not to. I put myself in this position because I thought I could handle it. I was overconfident in my recovery.

As the saying goes, "Pride goes before the fall," and I fell. I asked Jack to haul away debris we had from a remodeling project in his truck. It rained while we were loading the truck and our shirts got wet. Jack took off his shirt in the laundry room and I stared at him for a long time. I immediately thought of myself as a teenager and how similar we were in physique. Flashbacks of my abuse came flooding back and before I knew it, I was touching him inappropriately, the same way Father had touched me. I crossed the line. I felt ashamed and dirty and became engulfed in a dark sewer.

Jack left immediately and I started worrying, "What if he tells his parents or Marie what happened? What will Mary do when she finds out?" Almost instantly, I regressed to previous faulty patterns of thinking, "Forget it. It will go away! Don't say or do anything. It will be our secret." Fear took hold of me and made me sick inside. I remembered Mary saying, "If it happens again, I will leave you, and you will go to prison for a long time."

I didn't tell anyone. I worried constantly. Every time the phone rang, I jumped, thinking, "Someone has found out and is calling to tell Mary or Marie." I became nervous and edgy. I was short with family and friends. I isolated myself and became distant with Mary, withdrawing and spending my time in front of the television. I forgot the important things I had learned in SLAA. I wondered about Jack. Will this encounter affect him like it did me and change his life? I cried inside. Hurt and pain consumed me.

Part of me wanted to tell the truth; the other part of me was terrified thinking about the consequences—going to jail for a long time, losing Mary, my family and friends, and my job. Fear of publicity in the news and remembering all the pain and suffering of the past paralyzed me. I just couldn't handle telling Mary and the kids. I felt humiliated and a failure. I felt sick to my stomach, nervous, uneasy, and tense. I became depressed.

Marie's counselor felt it would be good for me to come with Mary for counseling. Mary wanted to start working on our marriage and restore some intimacy in our relationship. How could I face the counselor with my secret? How could I honestly communicate with Mary? I attempted to cooperate with the counselor, all the while carefully hiding my secret and the turmoil inside me.

Paul was in the seminary and Andrew was starting sixth grade. Tim was coming for dinner once a week, and Michael was busy planning his wedding fifteen hundred miles away. I didn't want to spoil everything.

Christmas and Michael's upcoming wedding, which normally would be times of intense celebration and joy, made me more depressed and lonely. I kept telling myself, "Don't ruin the wedding. Wait until afterwards." I experienced four months of hell and torture carrying the ugly secret inside me. Just before the wedding I got into an argument with Mary. I broke down and sobbed when she said, "You don't know *how* to love me." I wanted to tell her about my relapse, and I almost did, but once again I fought off the truth because of the wedding.

In January, the state patrol called and asked me to come to their office. They were investigating a report given them by a third party. They asked, "Did you touch this young man sexually in any way?"

"Yes," I answered. They gave me a ticket for third degree assault and a court date. Reality hit me. I couldn't keep it a secret any longer. I felt scared and frightened. I thought about running away and killing myself. I prayed for courage to go home and be open and honest with Mary. The Scripture, "The truth will set you free," kept coming to me.

Telling Mary was the hardest thing I have ever done. After lunch, I asked if we could talk. We went to our bedroom and sat on the bed. I said, "Do you remember when Marie's friend Jack was over? I had a relapse and abused him."

Mary looked stunned. She started sobbing, "How could you do it again? Why were you alone with Jack? You were just asking for trouble." Then she said the dreaded words, "I don't know if I can go through this again."

Mary was devastated. I worried, "Will she leave me? Will I go back to prison?" Memories of telling Mary twelve years earlier and all the pain that followed, came flooding into my mind. I felt a sense of relief because the secret was out, but at the same time, shame overwhelmed me and I feared what would happen next. Mary left immediately, saying she was going to church. Alone in the house, I replayed everything in my mind. Fear of jail and separation from the family haunted me.

Mary came home after two hours and said, "Father advised me to stay." She paused and held her breath. "I am not leaving you." I let out a sigh of relief.

It was devastating telling our children. Only Marie and Andrew were living at home. I was in the bedroom, down the hall, when Mary told Marie.

I heard her scream, "I hate him! I hate him! Why do you stay with him? Why don't you divorce him? I hate him!" She was angry and still reeling from the realization of my behavior years earlier. She wouldn't talk to me. She wouldn't even look at me. I couldn't blame her. I felt like the scum of the earth. Would she ever forgive me? The hurt and pain I caused pierced me to the core. I questioned my integrity—how could someone who is caring and loving do such bad things to hurt others?

Andrew came home from basketball practice, and Mary and I sat down with him at the kitchen table. Mary said, "Your dad had a relapse."

Andrew responded, "A what?" He obviously didn't understand. I tried to explain and mentioned what happened twelve years earlier before he was born.

Mary said, "Dad did it again." Andrew understood that.

I said, "I am so sorry, Andrew."

Mary hugged him and just held him while they both cried.

All I could do was fall down on my knees, recognize the wrong I had done, and beg for God's mercy and forgiveness. I cried until I could cry no more.

Mary

I was starting to understand Allan's problem as an addiction. Our relationship was strained from lack of intimacy and quality time together. Allan attended SLAA weekly, and I was involved in activities which nurtured my self-esteem and gave me an identity apart from being the wife of a child molester. I warned Allan many times that if he relapsed, the children and I would not go through all the pain again.

Michael's wedding was the day after Christmas, and we arrived several days earlier to help with preparations. Allan was especially irritable and emotional during this time. He seemed distant and distracted. He chose to attend Christmas Eve services by himself rather than stay home with the family. We fought about it, and Allan broke down in tears when I said he didn't really love me.

Tim added to the tension by informing us that he was gay. Wham! Another blow! Our joyous celebration was becoming a nightmare. Tim's statement didn't make any sense because he was attracted to beautiful women and didn't like men. Tim told us how a man propositioned him when he was helping at a homeless shelter. Tim reasoned that he must be gay if a man was attracted to him. This was the beginning of paranoia and irrational thinking caused by schizophrenia.

I put all our problems aside and enjoyed the time with Michael before his wedding. Allan's brother and his wife surprised us by showing up unannounced on Christmas Day. I almost fell over when I opened Michael's front door and saw them standing there. It touched us deeply that they drove so far. Michael and Elizabeth's wedding was beautiful. Elizabeth's family hosted a lavish reception and gave us a warm welcome.

Allan told me of his relapse shortly after we returned home. The horror I felt was devastating. I felt like a knife was thrust into my heart. The harsh voice of reality brought fear and anxiety for the future. Facts were coming out that I did not want to hear. Was it possible that my life would be totally turned upside down again? All the shame I felt before came flooding back. Knowing of Allan's own abuse and the nature of his addiction helped me to understand, but it didn't diminish the pain.

Immediately after Allan's disclosure, I went to church to pray and wait for my spiritual director. I couldn't deal with this myself. I poured out the whole story, and Father urged me to stay with Allan and see this through. I agreed only because I knew Father would help and support me. I knew that Jesus had said we are to forgive seventy times seven, and I'd grown enough to understand that forgiveness is not conditional or limited. So if I had truly forgiven Allan, then I had to forgive him again.

Michael and Elizabeth lived fifteen hundred miles away and Paul was in the seminary, so Allan's relapse would not directly impact their lives. Tim was diagnosed as mentally ill and was hospitalized for evaluation and treatment.

Marie was still in counseling. Allan's relapse, especially since it involved one of her friends, would be a major setback. Marie's new boyfriend, Luke, was an outstanding young man and willing to walk through all the pain with her. God brought him into Marie's life at a critical time, and Luke's love and affection eventually enabled her to forgive and let go of her bitterness.

Andrew, who was born while Allan was in prison, was now in sixth grade. Up to this point, he felt his relationship with his dad was pretty normal. He looked up to his dad but after we told him about the relapse, he had mixed emotions. He became very angry with his dad and hated what he had done. He was scared of what was going to happen to him and our family.

Probation

Allan

The lawyer was upset that I didn't contact him before meeting with the state patrol. Again, I was guilty and again I didn't want him trying to prove otherwise. The court date was scheduled for February but my lawyer wanted a different judge so the date was changed. At the last minute, my case was moved to yet another judge. Things did not look good. Changes at the last minute made my lawyer nervous.

I felt like I was headed for the slaughter. The fear of going back to prison was overwhelming. I didn't think I could do it again. I felt hopeless, but in this hopelessness, the only thing I could do was surrender and turn it all over to God. I just prayed, "I accept your will. Please give me and the family strength to get through this." I couldn't believe it when the judge sentenced me to two years probation. I was so relieved and grateful.

The probation officer explained exactly what was expected. I was to receive more intense counseling, a lie detector test, group sessions, extra SLAA meetings, and more accountability to my sponsor. The new counselor, who was an expert in sexual addiction, started an in-depth relapse program with me. I received individual counseling each week, in addition to attending group sessions.

During the next two years I began to understand the characteristics of denial and self-delusion and learned how to deal with confrontation. I learned about the addictive cycle and how to set boundaries and manage life without dysfunctional sexual behavior. We worked on shame reduction, family history, accountability, and crises management. I filled out detailed workbooks and weekly assignment sheets. As I completed them and gained more sobriety, I realized this was just the beginning of my recovery.

Mary and I attended *Parents United*, a program where perpetrators, adults abused as children, and parents of victims all come together in a controlled setting. I listened to victims tell their stories and express feelings of anger and shame. Their stories brought up feelings in me that I had buried. This program helped me to get in touch with my own abuse while feeling the pain I caused my victims.

Mary

Allan admitted his guilt when confronted by the state police, and surprisingly, they didn't arrest him but gave him a ticket requiring a court appearance. I was prepared for anything. All my dreams and expectations were shattered the first time Allan was arrested. This was like living a rerun and going through all the emotions again. The victim refused to press charges, so Allan's admission of guilt was all the prosecutor could use against him. The counselor and Allan's sponsor in SLAA wrote letters detailing Allan's current efforts at recovery. The judge was lenient and gave Allan two years probation rather than sending him to prison again. The requirements for probation were stringent and geared to making sure Allan became actively involved in his own recovery. Marie's counselor and the probation officer recommended the same counselor who specialized in sexual addiction. We met with the new counselor together two times, and then Allan started an intense program of weekly counseling and group sessions.

The lack of any intimacy in our marriage was one of the first issues addressed. She suggested that Allan get a good physical from an urologist to determine if the problem was physical or psychological. It turned out there was a physical problem which could easily be corrected with medicine. It was extremely difficult for me emotionally to resume intimacy with Allan after twelve years of avoiding it. I felt like I was on an altar being sacrificed rather than part of a loving union. There were so many feelings I had to deal with. I never refused Allan up to this point, and I wouldn't start now no matter how I felt.

I started attending group sessions given by Allan's counselor for wives of sex addicts. After listening to the other wives, I realized how unusual it was to have a husband who wanted to be healed and change his behavior. The husbands of the other wives in the group were angry and resistant to counseling, making the wives suspicious and fearful. I was concerned about Allan, but I didn't spend my time worrying about his every move. Allan agreed to my suggestion that we pray together and he willingly accompanied me to Marie's counselor. It wasn't until I heard from the other wives, how bad things could be that I appreciated Allan's openness and cooperation.

We also attended *Parents United*, a program which brought sex offenders, adults abused as children, and parents of victims all together in discussion groups. Victims were not placed in groups with perpetrators until they had attended at least thirteen weeks. I was placed in a group with victims and parents of victims. After hearing the victims' stories, it took me all week to recover emotionally. I was in a difficult place—my heart was breaking for the victims, and yet I was married to an offender. These sessions engulfed me in shame and disgust for what Allan had done.

Andrew went to a children's program run by *Parents United*. They placed him in a group of victims around his own age. It was a real eye opener for Andrew, and he matured tremendously during the twelve weeks he attended. Andrew developed excellent listening skills and empathy for other kids who were hurting. He used these skills in his relationships with friends and classmates. At the end of junior high, Andrew was selected by his classmates to receive the school's spirit award which was given to the student who they felt was encouraging, loyal, spirited, and dedicated. It was a great honor.

Becoming Whole

Allan

After my relapse, Mary felt I needed deep spiritual healing so the roots of my sexual addiction could be healed. I agreed because my relapse showed I still had a problem. She asked a prayer community if they would pray with me. They gave us the name of Tom and Betty Brown who agreed to meet with us. The first time we went for prayer I felt uncomfortable and fought it. But the unconditional love I felt after Tom and Betty listened to our story and prayed with us helped me relax and let go of my fears. They arranged to pray with me every week for at least an hour while I continued counseling and attending SLAA.

After a few sessions, small changes began to happen. I still had tremendously low self-esteem. Tom and Betty said, "You always hold your head down in shame, even when you are praying." They encouraged me to "look at God" when I prayed. He loved me. He wasn't ashamed of me but hurt whenever I hurt. They spoke of my dignity as God's child—not because I could ever do anything to earn God's love but because God loved me unconditionally.

I knew I was powerless. I needed God! I had to do the work but God's grace was needed to allow my mind and heart to change. For once, my thinking was clear, and I felt ready and open to receive God's love for me. I made a decision to change. Tom and Betty encouraged me to look people in the eye when I talked to them. It was difficult to do this. I usually looked to the side or down at the floor because I felt so unworthy, but they said God loved me, as did a lot of other people.

At my next SLAA meeting, I noticed that everyone was looking down at the floor as they prayed. We all felt so much shame that it seemed we couldn't come before God and believe He accepted us.

I kept all this in the back of my mind and slowly started "looking at God" when I prayed and made an effort to look people in the eye when I talked to them. For the first time, I didn't feel like I was the lowest guy on the totem pole, and over time, I was able to stand up for my opinions in any kind of confrontation. In the past I would freeze and run from even the smallest disagreement. Now I was able to be honest and speak what was truly on my mind, and my self esteem improved. The people-pleaser Allan was being replaced by the real me. I was on the road to true recovery.

One time as Tom and Betty prayed, I had an image of being in a group of people but with a bag over my head and feeling all alone. I was always terrified of being alone and isolated. I took the bag off my head and saw that I wasn't alone. I wasn't alone! This awareness made all the difference in the world. I experienced this same feeling at my first SLAA meeting—initially feeling I was the only one who had this terrible addiction, and then finding out that I wasn't alone.

Through the prayer sessions, I soon realized I was in a spiritual war. I always referred to my feelings and behavior as "my condition." After many months of prayer, I recognized that it was sin and Satan that I battled, not my condition or addiction. Before I assumed this was how I was and how I would always be—kind of like being stuck in a block of cement with no hope of ever being freed. In fact, I never thought breaking free from these thoughts and feelings was a possibility; I just thought I would be trapped forever. This awareness of the truth encouraged me, and I stopped listening to the thoughts that supported my addictive behaviors. I began to replace the craziness with healthy thinking and activities.

For example, at times I heard my addiction (Satan) say, "You should treat yourself by masturbating. It will take away the stress you are under. It will make you feel better. It's OK to sexualize young males; you're not hurting anyone else." I learned to stop these thoughts immediately and counter them with thoughts about the preciousness of each human being and the sacredness of my own body. When I would see a teenage boy, I would remind myself that he could be my son.

Gradually I began to feel something different happening deep inside me. I couldn't explain it at first. But as I learned more about myself and what was true, it was like the bag of isolation was removed. No more secrets and no more leading two lives. The more we prayed, the closer I came to God and the less I listened to Satan and his lies about me. My addiction's—or rather sin and Satan's—hold on me was starting to lose its grip. Positive and true thoughts replaced negative thoughts. As I prayed, sacrificed, and put God first in my life, things started happening. I looked deeper into my background, family history, and sexual abuse and started dealing with the issues in my life that I had repressed and kept deep inside me.

At this time, I participated in a group of men and women who were abused as children. This was an intense experience and repressed memories of my abuse came forth along with the feelings I had suppressed. For the first time I started to *feel*.

I faced nagging questions that I had previously ignored. "Was there something the matter with me that Fr. Walker was attracted to me? Was I gay? Did the abuse happen because I wasn't good enough?" These issues came up, and I prayed about them. Hidden underneath all my feelings all these years was the lie that said I was the cause of my abuse. But it wasn't my fault that I had been abused! Slowly I began to believe the truth that the abuse I experienced as a teenager wasn't my fault. Through counseling and prayer, I started to feel again. I was told many times that it was not the victim's fault but the fault of the abuser—and for the first time I could believe it. The truth—IT WASN'T MY FAULT that I had been abused—started to set me free.

Another area that needed healing was having permission and the right to have feelings. In the group of victims, each of us had been abused, but I was the only one who was also a perpetrator. This made me feel like disappearing. There was a teenage girl, Sue, in the group who had been abused by her father. She was extremely hostile towards all men. Through the rough treatment I received from her—the glaring stares and the loud yelling aimed at me—I was pushed to my limit. I finally shouted, "I HAVE FEELINGS TOO!" This sticking up for myself (and even my feelings!) was new and frightening at first, but it was also freeing. I didn't shutdown and deny my feelings but was able to open up and experience healing.

I shared with Sue and the whole group, admitting I had done something horrible that I wished I could undo but I couldn't. Now I was ready to accept and face the consequences for what I had done. I was ready to make amends for my actions. Sue listened to me and came to realize that perpetrators are human beings with feelings, too. After that, our group was much more supportive of each other and became more trusting and open.

As I began to heal emotionally, mentally, and spiritually, I came to a deeper realization of how much I needed God's help. I couldn't do it myself. Gone was the double life that I once led where I appeared happy-go-lucky on the outside while feeling angry and hurting on the inside. Now the peace and joy I felt internally radiated to the surface.

Soon after these realizations, I found that offering my struggles and temptations to God and letting Him take care of them worked. This didn't mean I didn't have to do anything but rather I worked harder than ever disciplining myself to do my best and to trust God. I was tapping into God's tremendous graces, mercy, and help.

Tom and Betty encouraged me to start writing my thoughts and feelings to God each day. I do not like to write. I was never a good speller and found it difficult expressing my true feelings and thoughts on paper, so I resisted. When I went to pray with them, I conveniently "forgot" my journal at home.

At this same time, some people in my therapy share group started journaling with positive results in their lives. This encouraged me to at least give it a try. At first, I only journaled a few words two or three times a week. Months later, my journaling increased and I wrote a few sentences. One of my problems with journaling was making the time to do it. It's always easy to find time for things you want to do, but I didn't want to do this. I found it hard to express my thoughts and feelings, making journaling extremely difficult work for me. I was still trying to figure out who the real me was and what I felt and thought, and journaling helped identify this for me. By the end of a year, I could sometimes fill a whole page.

Even though daily journaling was still a struggle, I started to see how God was leading and healing me. Often His great love overwhelmed me. At first, I had a real fear that someone who knew me would read my journal, but as I healed and my journaling reflected who I really was, this fear went away. In fact, eventually Mary and I started to share our journals with each other each evening.

Together, the combination of counseling and journaling helped me understand how my inner feelings had an effect on my body physically. For example, when I became angry or stressed, my neck and stomach muscles tightened, and I sweated more. I had never recognized the connection between the two. I remember getting frustrated over the kids turning the stereo too loud and yelling at them—but later I understood the true cause of my outburst. It wasn't the loud music but the unresolved disagreement I had with Mary the previous night. Gradually I realized that the way my body felt and how I reacted to things, gave me clues as to what was going on deep inside me.

In counseling, I learned that when I was in a situation where I came in contact with a teenage boy, I was to write down the situation, my thoughts, feelings, and whether they were addictive or constructive. In addition, I was to record any actions that I took after these thoughts. Doing this, along with journaling, helped me realize that sexual attraction to teenage boys was an effort to gain power over the trauma of my own abuse. Once this connection was made, the disordered attraction greatly diminished. Now I could identify thoughts and feelings that would potentially lead me to destructive behavior. Writing it down on paper allowed me to see that my old addictive thinking was changing and being replaced by new, healthy thoughts.

Mary

Our marriage needed tremendous healing and so did I. I wanted more. As I watched the kind of relationships our children had with their chosen partners, I felt jealous. I wanted a marriage with intimacy, honest communication, and unconditional love. Also I was afraid if Allan didn't receive deep inner healing, he could face another relapse. That was unthinkable.

I called a local prayer community and asked if they would pray with us. They prayed and discerned. We were assigned to a wonderful couple. Allan and I went together the first time, and although we had never met this couple, we immediately sensed their unconditional love for us. They spent an hour every week praying with each of us separately. During these sessions, we shared a little and they prayed, asking God's direction and healing for us. We developed a deep level of trust with them.

After several weeks, I was able to lessen my prayer sessions—at first going every other week, then monthly. Allan continued to attend weekly. Periodically Allan and I went together, and gradually the walls between us began to melt away.

Through prayer and God's grace, everything began to change. I started to see some hope. As Tom and Betty continued praying with me, God's love came alive and through His love, my heart opened to Allan. I was able to see Allan through God's eyes and experience God's love for him. I saw that God was not judging Allan but had compassion and love for him. I saw how precious Allan was to God, and through God's eyes of love for Allan, I took a good long look at how I had been treating him. I had been treating him in a demeaning way, almost like he was one of the kids needing direction. I was very controlling.

Realizing this, I felt very remorseful. I wondered if my actions had made matters worse all these years. The Lord gave me a glimpse of how much even the little things we do affect others; how our actions either build others up or tear them down. This realization was brought home to me early one morning on a trip. Ice covered our car, so Allan told me to wait in the lobby while he scraped the windows. It was cold and dark. I was getting impatient because it was taking so long. Finally, Allan drove around. The windshield wiper had come off, and he had struggled to fix it in the dark. Flashbacks came to me of Allan giving up in frustration when he tried to build or fix something. At these times, I jumped in and showed him that I could do it. Sometimes I didn't even give him a chance. We would be working on a project together, and I would just take over. Allan would back off and retreat to safer territory. This memory pierced my heart—it brought to life how I treated Allan, putting him down and finding fault rather than pointing out all the things about him that were right.

As disillusionment with our marriage set in, I had retreated into my own selfishness, wanting things my way, not even taking Allan's wants or feelings into consideration. I was destroying any belief he might have in himself. My inability to encourage and build-up Allan's self-confidence was magnified right before my eyes. Why was I like this? Why was it so hard for me to encourage him? I always felt that I had to have everything under control and prove that I was good enough. I acted as if God kept track of what I did right and where I failed. I wanted to be perfect and prove that I was worthy of love. I wasn't able to accept God's unconditional love.

The perception that I was only worthwhile and loveable when I was productive and doing the "right thing" fed into my struggles with food. If I ate something that wasn't "legal", I would feel guilty and end up eating more to feel better. I overachieved to compensate for my failures in developing intimate relationships. I felt like a bulldozer who lacked the sensitivity and gentleness that I admire in people who are socially at ease and make others feel so special.

I treated Allan as if he had to prove he was a worthwhile person too. I needed to learn what unconditional love was. I didn't have to do anything to prove I was worthy of being loved, and Allan didn't need to prove himself worthy either. When I could accept God's love for me and put aside the notion that I had to be perfect, only then would I be able to accept Allan and others the way they were, and see them in the light of God's overwhelming love for them.

Now I saw that all these years I had been reinforcing Allan's negative childhood messages that he didn't quite measure up. My natural abilities and impatience were detrimental to our relationship. For the first time in our marriage, I wanted to change this. After Allan's arrest it was easy to blame all our problems on him, but now I had to face my own selfishness and lack of love. I certainly wasn't perfect, and my own battle with impatience and overeating constantly reminded me of this.

In one of our sessions, Tom and Betty suggested that I learn how to play and have down time with Allan. I wasn't even aware that I forgot how to have fun. I was always busy and worrying about everything that needed to be done. Tom and Betty pointed out that Allan knew how to relax and play a lot better than I did, so I could learn from him. Allan and I started by going for a walk in the woods together and having a picnic. The sunlight on the leaves warmed my heart and brought me great peace. Next we went to the park and Allan pushed me on the swings. I felt like a little girl again. These simple things made me hopeful that we could really grow in love.

Through prayer and Allan's sharing, I got a glimpse into Allan's inner self and true feelings. I could see the young boy who felt awkward and intimidated by those who bullied him. He wanted to be accepted for who he was. Allan shared his fear of being unable to perform sexually. Understanding this made a huge difference in how I saw Allan. I opened up to Allan and began trusting him again.

We started to read our prayer journals to each other every night, and this helped us develop intimacy at a much deeper level. Allan's healing was reaching into the core of who he was, showing him that he was a beloved child of God. He became open to new ideas. The defensive walls he had built up around himself began to fall away. This didn't happen overnight. It wasn't until we looked back after a year of praying, journaling, and sharing with each other on a daily basis that we saw the progress.

New Perspective

Allan

I am changing and growing. Today I think about the changes which will help prevent my past behavior. Before I tried to control my actions out of fear—white knuckling it. The roots of my sexual addiction were still embedded deep inside me even though the visible part was gone. Through the victim group, sexual addiction counseling, prayer, and journaling these roots have been dug up and removed. The desire to act out sexually is gone, and I quickly deal with occasional thoughts and temptations to act out by turning my mind to healthy alternatives.

I have much stronger self-esteem based on God's love for me, and I am not afraid to share my true self and feelings. I am relaxed and can make mistakes. Now I learn from them rather than becoming frustrated and angry. I feel confident and happy in my ability to express my true feelings and thoughts. This is a huge change from my past behavior of stuffing everything inside me. I have more compassion for others and do not judge their actions. God has forgiven me and I certainly must do the same for others.

My thoughts are clearer now and more positive. I am free from the darkness of sexual abuse, both as victim and as abuser. I am free of the anger I carried for so long, the anger that sapped my energy and made me a walking pressure cooker ready to explode. Gone is the secret I carried and guarded each day. Life can still be stressful, and I still get angry at times, but I have learned to deal with stress in a healthy way and talk about what's bothering me. I can handle responsibility and make good decisions for our family. I have never been healthier emotionally and spiritually.

I can never say that I am totally healed. I will always have to guard against slipping back into past ways of thinking and behaving. I presently chair a twelve-step group and have taken on the role of sponsorship, reaching out to other men and women with sexual addiction. By helping others and giving back to the community, I see myself growing in love, joy and serenity.

In addition to praying with Mary, I have developed a daily prayer routine of my own. In the morning, I read "The Serenity Prayer" and meditate for fifteen minutes. This focuses me for the day. After work, I read Scripture, listen in the quiet of my heart, and journal my thoughts and feelings.

With my mind clear and the spiritual strength I received through prayer, I started honestly communicating with Mary at a whole new level. We share our journals each night, reading to each other what we wrote during the day. This sharing and praying together has made us stronger as a couple and improved our communication. Not being in touch with our own feelings or sharing them was a huge part of the problem in the past. We never knew how each other really felt. Before going to bed, Mary and I reflect on the positive and negative things that happened throughout the day. I go to sleep thinking of the things that give me life and increased love in my heart.

I reached a milestone when I was able to share with Mary my fears and feelings about having sex and not being a complete man. Since she knew my secret, I told her how the abuse made me feel dirty and unworthy of her love. Sharing our feelings allowed us to know each other at a deeper level and be more compassionate of each other's struggles and feelings. Our love grows stronger as emotional intimacy deepens.

Mary and I started dating again and having fun. We enjoy walking while holding hands or just sitting together on the swing in our backyard. We take time to reconnect in our busy, stressful world by going away together for the weekend. A retreat center nestled amongst trees near a lazy river is one of our favorite getaways.

I feel peace and joy as I reconnect with God, Mary, and my family. Jesus has become my friend, not just a historical person. I never knew how far I had drifted away from God emotionally and spiritually since my abuse forty-four years ago. I am constantly and diligently working on my spiritual growth. With continued prayer and God's grace, I will cross the bridge and become whole.

I now live a life committed to a loving relationship with Mary. She is not only my wife but also my best friend. I can come to her and share any part of myself. There are no more hidden secrets or lies. We can experience who Allan and Mary really are. I enjoy just being around my wife. We share our gifts and talents together and grow from them.

Recently we worked together with our son, Paul, to redo a friend's kitchen. We enjoyed working side-by-side. In the past, especially when it came to mechanical tasks, Mary would get upset because I took so long. This time, we recognized and appreciated each other's talents and enjoyed doing it together.

Today my relationship with Mary is much closer and at a deeper level than ever before in our thirty-five years of marriage. Mary and I truly celebrate the sacrament of marriage that has united us.

New Vision

Mary

*"How do I see you, O Lord?
Do I see You as a loving God who calls me deeper and deeper into
intimacy with Himself?
What I fear is my own wretchedness and sinfulness,
yet You keep calling and calling me
closer and closer to You."*

Entry from Mary's Journal

God has given me the gift of seeing Allan with new eyes. I see the beauty of my husband and am able to appreciate his gentleness and humility. His patience and confidence that God will take care of things help balance my tendency to worry and be anxious. Instead of becoming upset, I relax and let go more easily now if something isn't done perfectly or right away.

Allan has taught me to really see and enjoy the beauty around me, like the vibrant colors of nature and the miracle of a flower or a tree. The little love notes he leaves on my pillow or puts in the bag I take to work help me to feel treasured. Now when he brings me roses, I am really grateful and see the gift of his heart. This is a big change from when we were first married, when I would get upset that he spent so much money on something that was just going to die.

Allan is very sensitive to my moods. If I am down or struggling with something, he is quick to sense it. He doesn't try to fix me. He just listens and encourages me. Allan will take a lot of time looking for just the right card, and if he sees something that he thinks would be a great present for someone, he will get it even if there is no special occasion.

I especially appreciate Allan's patience in dealing with our oldest son, Tim. When Tim was finishing his last class for an associate's degree, he had a major setback in his battle with paranoid schizophrenia. Tim lives with us and requires a tremendous amount of patience and sensitivity. Through Allan's support, I have been able to see Tim as a gift in our lives.

I am not the same person I was before Allan's arrest. Things are no longer black and white. In the past, I was judgmental and narrow. Something was either right or wrong (and my way was always the right way). I've learned to open my eyes and see possibilities that I never knew existed before. Now I stop and take time to appreciate life and look at it through other people's eyes. I do not judge or condemn the actions of another person. A new compassion for others is developing deep within me that allows me to see people the way Jesus sees them. Jesus came to bring life, not to judge or to condemn—and I want to bring life, too. I want to bring forgiveness and help others see how precious they are in God's eyes, no matter what they have done.

I now realize that my fears and the smallness of my understanding of God's love and mercy kept me stunted spiritually. I see how my rigidity in thinking everything had to be perfect prevented me from receiving the fullness of God's love, and it prevented me from giving and receiving love from others, too. I was more concerned with my unworthiness than responding to the gift of love that was being offered.

I try to live in the present moment and see what is there, right where I am, looking at it and appreciating it. If my plans get disrupted and changed, it doesn't throw me for a loop like it once did. The need to be perfect has been replaced by a calmer acceptance of my own humanity, my messiness, my own weakness, and my selfishness. I have a deeper realization that God can take the failings and tragedies of my life and weave a tapestry that is made perfect in His plan.

I realize just how special and unique each person is, and I enjoy the gift they are in my life. I see the inside of a person—the pain, the struggles, and the frustrations that are often hidden but still part of their lives. I see the messiness of our human condition, and I look on others with compassion as they struggle to find God's unique plan for their lives. It doesn't have to be my plan or the way I would do things.

This letting go is hardest with my own children. I have so many dreams and hopes for them. I don't want them to experience the pain I have been through, but they are on their own journey of faith and must discover the reality of God for themselves in their own way.

How much God loves each of us just the way we are! With this new understanding, I have been truly humbled and changed forever. I have encountered the living God who waits for me every minute of every hour because He knows me so intimately and loves me so fiercely. I am grateful He is the kind of God who doesn't allow me to go my own merry way but allows trials and suffering so that He can break through the hard shell of my heart. My relationship with Allan couldn't begin to heal until I acknowledged my own sinfulness and was able to seek forgiveness.

My heart is open to greater love now, and I can honestly say I am grateful for Allan and the gift he has been in my life. Since he has been set free and enabled to love, I have experienced his gentle and unconditional love for me. For the first time I see Allan as a lover—and a real-life partner. He brings fun into my life. Before trying to get Allan to share his feelings was so difficult; he was very superficial—always kidding and funny, but he never got into a discussion about feelings or anything serious. I didn't know him at all. Now I can appreciate him as a person, and I look forward to spending time with him.

Now I enjoy working with Allan, whereas before I preferred working by myself.

Tom and Betty strongly encouraged us to write down our story. After praying, Allan and I both felt this was God's will. Writing this book has been very painful and difficult, but it has also been very healing. Remembering and pondering our life has given me deep gratitude and joy for God's mercy and all the miracles that transformed our family. It is like giving birth to a child. We experience extreme suffering during the birth, but it is followed by joy that a new life has been born. Life itself is like that if we are faithful to God's will. Sorrow and suffering will be followed by joy in the Lord. I thank God for the pain in my life. It has transformed me into a kinder, more gentle, and loving person, and pain continues to soften and change me every day.

We have weathered additional storms in the past few years, which rather than divide us, have brought us closer together. Allan was diagnosed with prostate cancer two years ago. I realized how much I would miss him if he died. This is a big change. I used to think that if something happened to Allan, it would hardly faze me and I would just keep going. Now I know I would feel a huge emptiness in my life. I would really miss him. I love Allan so much more and in a much deeper way than when we were first married. We were faced with making a decision on which course of treatment to pursue to treat his cancer. This was difficult because all the choices had severe drawbacks. We decided on radical surgery which was followed by a long period of recovery. Allan is still experiencing physical problems due to the surgery.

During Allan's recovery, Tim had a major relapse and was forced to withdraw from school. The doctor could not find a medication that worked effectively and resorted to shock treatments. Tim rarely left the house for over a year and at one point we feared he would have to be institutionalized. After a recent hospitalization, we changed doctors and started a new medication regimen that is showing positive results. Tim now attends a program designed to help him lead a more productive life by teaching coping and behavior skills

Also during this past year, Allan's Aunt Maggie died at the age of ninety-five. After the funeral, we shared with Allan's brother and his wife all that happened in our lives. *No more secrets*! They were stunned. A lot of gnawing questions were answered, and they were sad that Aunt Maggie kept it from them. Our openness allowed them to share with us on a deeper level and opened the door to a whole new dimension in our relationship.

New Life

Allan and Mary

We are writing this last chapter together with deep gratitude to God for all He has done in our lives and marriage. Only God could take the ashes of our lives and make something beautiful. We are always taken aback when someone who does not know where we have been, comes up to us in church and says what an example of love and unity our family is to them.

We recently celebrated our thirty-fifth wedding anniversary by renewing our wedding vows and exchanging rings. The prongs on Mary's diamond were breaking and the jeweler advised us to replace the head. Allan lost his wedding band many years ago, so we decided to take Mary's wedding band and have it resized for Allan. We picked out a new wrap around band for Mary and waited until the ceremony to exchange our new rings.

We pledged our vows and exchanged rings, not with the idealism of a young bride and groom, but with the experience of years of pain and struggle. We chose to be committed to each other and to God while being fully aware that married life isn't easy. We were choosing to say "Yes, we will stay together and love, honor, and obey each other despite what may come."

The result of all these changes in our lives flows over into the level of intimacy we experience together. Allan's abuse as a teen and addiction built up walls that made true intimacy impossible until God's healing power penetrated that barrier. We now enjoy a deep emotional and spiritual intimacy that overshadows physical intimacy as we grow older. Interestingly, we learned some of the lessons about intimacy from our children. When Marie and Luke, and Paul and Corrinne were courting, we felt jealous. They seemed to be so much in love and were constantly showing little signs of affection. They talked for hours and never seemed to be bored with each other. They modeled healthy relationships for us, and we watched and learned.

Some of those nonverbal ways of communicating love are now part of our lives. As we grow together we now enjoy just being together, holding hands, listening to music, reading, or watching a good movie.

On a weekend getaway recently, Allan surprised me (Mary) by bringing some shrimp and wine along with a present of body lotion and bath accessories. After we toasted our future, Allan gave me (Mary) a wonderful foot rub. This was the first time Allan had ever done this, and I was deeply moved by his tenderness and love. We no longer look longingly at the relationships of our children with their spouses because we realize that we have a deeper, more mature love than is possible for newly married couples. Our relationship is characterized by gentleness and a mutual understanding that is the fruit of acceptance.

The spiritual journey we were on separately has come together through the sharing of our journals. In addition to our individual prayer time, we pray together for half an hour each morning and again before retiring at night. We both find that when we are separated, it is much harder to say the rosary. We are so used to saying it together that it feels like a part of our body is missing when we say it alone.

Each evening we try to identify the moment for which we are most grateful and also what left us feeling empty and estranged from God or each other. This usually leads to further discussion of why we chose those particular moments. It has been a great way to share our feelings on a daily basis.

We belong to a Marriage Encounter sharing group with five other wonderful couples who have accepted and loved us even when we couldn't love ourselves or each other. Their love and support have helped us to see how precious we are as a couple. They have helped us to see our sacrament of marriage as a sign of how Christ loves His Church. Our love and forgiveness of each other is a witness of God's love and forgiveness.

God has brought unity to our marriage in other more mundane areas also. A couple of years ago we embarked on a spiritual growth weight loss program together. We learned to eat much smaller portions, and Allan lost fifteen pounds just prior to being diagnosed with cancer. This weight loss was a great asset for his recovery from surgery. The spiritual part of this program, which emphasized sacrifice and discipline, has helped us grow together. Mary really admired the discipline and virtue Allan developed in his eating, and Mary learned to eat according to hunger and no longer ate huge quantities of so-called diet foods. Now when we go out to eat, we order one meal and share it together. Because we are healthier and have more energy, we are able to enjoy walking and bike riding together.

Another fruit of our growth has been the development of a budget. Previously we were afraid to look at where our money was going. In the past we had budgets—we just didn't follow them. Allan had a bad habit of spending money foolishly; spending money made him feel in control. Mary, on the other hand, was the prudent one in the family and more budget-minded. Due to these differences, dealing with finances was always stressful. God always provided for us financially, but we realized we needed to do our part and use our resources according to His will. Now because of the change within him, Allan doesn't feel the need to spend excessively. Sticking to the budget has required each of us to put aside our own selfish desires and work together for the good of the whole family.

In the past, Christmas holidays were always a time of tension between us. Mary became upset over all the Christmas decorations Allan bought, which he put up earlier and earlier each year. Mary felt the season of Advent was ignored, and we jumped from Thanksgiving right into Christmas. Our garage and precious storage space under the steps were always crowded with Christmas decorations. As our relationship improved, Mary entered into Allan's childlike anticipation of Christmas and actually enjoyed holiday preparations and decorating. This past Christmas we spent three hours together driving around until we found the perfect Christmas tree. In the past, Mary would have settled for the first tree we found just to get it over with. This time we kept looking until we came to a Christmas tree farm in the middle of nowhere. Once we found the right tree, we cut it down ourselves. It was bitterly cold, and we got lost trying to find our way back to the main highway, but it was so much fun sharing the experience together. We brought the tree home and put blue lights and an angel on it for the Advent season, and just before Christmas we added the rest of the decorations. Christmas was so much more joyful when we were united and able to appreciate each other's point of view. God didn't make us the same. He wanted an endless variety of flowers in His garden, and we are learning to appreciate the uniqueness of each other and the qualities those differences bring to our relationship.

God truly has restored all the years the locust has eaten. This is not a scholarly work. We are ordinary, sinful people whom God has showered with His mercy and love. We will be eternally grateful. The book is ending, but our story continues to be written in the daily fabric of our lives, and the lives of our children and grandchildren. Only in Heaven will the final beauty of that tapestry be seen.

Our story is one of hope, hope that no matter how dark the situation, no matter how much pain there is, God's love and mercy can and will be victorious if we turn to Him. All God needs to bring good out of evil is our obedience and perseverance. As we look back on the tragedies and triumphs of our lives, we see how God was with us at each step, with each tear, amidst the darkness and confusion, in every circumstance whether we were aware of His presence and love or not. To families who are struggling with crises in their own lives, we say, "Do not lose hope! Do not surrender to the darkness and succumb to the pain! Morning always follows the night. God always provides a way out for us—if only we persevere. He always sends people into our lives who love and sustain us. Reach out to those who are reaching out to you. You are not alone. You do not have to do it all by yourself."

Our own story has taught us that it is impossible to survive without help. In fact, our story is not only our own, but the story of all those who journeyed with us along the way. To them we offer our heartfelt thanks. Most especially to God, we want to offer our deepest and most profound praise. Nothing is impossible with Him. Nothing is possible without Him. Our very lives are a testament to that basic and unalterable truth.

Epilogue: The Family Room

We are including current information and reflections from each of our children.

Tim

Tim continues to improve. He enjoys walking in the woods and listening to music. In addition, he keeps our lawn mowed and dishwasher emptied.

Tim's Reflection

I was very sad when I found out my dad molested one of my friends. He went to jail for a year. This happened when I was in the seventh grade. This is a difficult time in a kid's life, and my dad being away from our family for a year made things that much worse. I missed my dad and was angry that he had disappeared from our lives. One day after he came home, I punched my dad because I blamed all the problems in my life on him. I was dealing with undiagnosed schizophrenia, which was to become worse as I got older. I realized later that I was responsible for my own problems, and they were not my dad's fault. I will always regret punching my dad. Today my dad is one of my best friends. When I am well enough, we go out to eat together, go shopping, and watch movies. God has blessed me with a great dad.

Michael

Michael and his wife Elizabeth live on the East Coast and have three daughters. Michael owns a successful business that recently expanded to our state, enabling him to visit more often. Elizabeth has a degree in theater and is a wonderful mother. In addition to caring for their children and home, she helps Michael with his business and does volunteer work with children's theater and dance groups. We visit them twice a year and they try to come for several days at Thanksgiving.

Michael's Reflection

I love all of our family very much. Having gone through what we did, I feel we have a very special bond. The Lord has blessed us in many ways and has a special place for all of us. I have forgiven Dad completely and have a better understanding for his addiction and what happened. I also realize, from his relapse, that it is an ongoing struggle.

The difficulties I experienced because of dad's crime strengthened my relationship and appreciation for God and my family. Before all this happened, I was an overly confident, cocky kid. Dad's arrest and imprisonment brought me down to the lowest point ever. But amazingly, it taught me how to love people. It made me more understanding, forgiving, and humble. I learned the value of hard work and perseverance. I became an all-round better person.

Paul

Paul decided to try the seminary after his sophomore year of college. After a year, he discerned that the priesthood was not his vocation and returned to pursuing a career in engineering. He met Corrine, an education major, while in college. Paul graduated, found an excellent job, and married Corrine the following year. Corrine gladly gave up teaching to be a stay-at-home mom. They now have two children.

Paul's Reflection

As I got older, I understood and appreciated the sacrifice, suffering and perseverance of my mother and father. I stand in awe of the relationship my parents have now. Not only have they healed, but their relationship has improved tremendously as a result of their suffering and hard work. I appreciate my father much more now than ever before. I notice more of his good qualities such as generosity, charity, meekness, humility, and patience. Because of him, I am more compassionate and sensitive toward others and understand adverse addictions.

I feel that our family is very tight-knit and supportive. I especially enjoy our Sunday family dinners together. We are avid game players and enjoy a variety of board and card games. When the weather is good, we have a competitive game of croquet where the loser has to do the dishes or treat everyone to Dairy Queen. We also enjoy playing baseball and basketball and have had a great game of football in the snow.

Marie

Marie is a nurse and married her high school sweetheart, Luke. Luke completed his master's in engineering just as their first baby girl arrived. Marie was delighted to trade dispensing pills and needles for diapers. Corrine and Marie enjoy letting the cousins play together and participating in a mom's group. Luke and Marie also attend a bi-weekly Bible study group with Paul and Corrine and several other couples.

Marie's Reflection

Faith, along with time and maturity, helped me heal from the pain my Dad made so real for me. Luke's love gave me a glimpse of Christ's love for me and made me want to share that love with others. God gave me Luke and his family at just the right time. He gave me the grace I needed to find Christ and to know I needed to make Him the center of my life in a very personal way. Christ loved all of us so much that He gave His life for us, and I know He did that for me and for my Dad. Christ forgave my Dad and calls me to do the same. I began to see that all people have value. I also realized that value is not based on what people can do or what they can contribute, but is based on the mere fact that they are human beings created in the image and likeness of God. God loves them so much. Knowing that helped me to have a real compassion for people who are not treated with dignity. It also helped me to not only forgive my dad, but myself and my own shortcomings. Knowing my own value was not based on what I accomplished in life helped, and continues to help me, when I struggle with low self-esteem.

My dad and mom both walked me down the aisle when I married my sweetheart Luke. My dad and I danced to an Irish song called "Dance with Me, Daughter." My dad's heritage to me is to truly learn from people, that everyone has something to give, and you must be humble.

Today I enjoy getting together with my family. I have such a deep respect for my mom for dealing with all she did, and then not only sticking it out with my Dad but really working on their marriage to make it what God created it to be. I can tell she loves my Dad, and I can tell from where she has been that there is nothing my Dad can do to lose that love. What a lesson so many people could use. And I was able to witness it firsthand. That is truly how Christ loves us.

I also respect my dad and admire him for working so hard to carry his cross. He does it with such joy and humility. He is someone who knows how to reach out in love to people that are in need. He has such a compassion for the "underdogs" of this world. By his actions, He has taught me to love those who are hardest to love because they probably need it the most. There is still some baggage that goes along with me, but Luke has accepted me and works at it with me. I know that Christ can use me to do His work if I allow myself to be open to His grace. Love truly does cover a multitude of sins.

Andrew

Andrew is in college majoring in psychology and philosophy. He plays the guitar and leads a very active social life in addition to keeping up with his studies.

Andrew's Reflections

I was born while my dad was in prison. The earlier incident didn't affect me as much as the rest of the family. My relationship with my dad was pretty normal until sixth grade. His relapse drastically changed that. He was humbled to the point where he had almost no parental authority. It was hard to show him love and respect. I often disregarded his requests. There was a lot of tension between my dad and me during middle school. I grouped little things he did that annoyed me with his problem and I was irritable and unforgiving.

I didn't think much about what happened during high school because it affected me less and less. I looked up to my brother, Paul, and my sister's husband, Luke. They exemplified what a Christian man should be and became my new role models. They helped me understand the importance of forgiveness and loving people unconditionally.

As I mature, my relationship with my dad grows closer every year. I love and respect him for many things, but especially for his courage and humility. When I think of charity, I think of my dad. My parents have shown me what true commitment involves. Their perseverance has resulted in a close-knit family that really enjoys being together and helping each other. I love my family and savor the time we spend together.

Appendix A: Mary's Research Paper

Mary wrote the following research paper for an English Class in 1990. This is the paper we sent to Fr. Walker. It is exactly as it was written in 1990 and does not reflect the most current information.

Sexual Abuse of Boys: Its Pervasive Effects

When a newspaper article tells the story of child sexual abuse, it usually focuses on the perpetrator. Rarely is anything mentioned about the victim. Books and the media have only recently revealed information about the psychological and emotional trauma to the victim, usually female. However, even more recently, the secrecy surrounding sexual abuse of young boys in American society is beginning to be broken. Sexual abuse can involve direct contact (overt) or nondirect, emotionally damaging behavior (covert).

The emotional and psychological damage done when a young boy is sexually molested will pervade every area of his adult life unless it is dealt with and healing occurs. The traumatizing experience of sexual abuse will cause the victim to shut down emotionally, be unable to develop normal intimate relationships, become shame-based, and be at high risk of becoming a sex addict. Organizations and support groups are available to facilitate healing of the male victim by helping him through the necessary grieving process and teaching new behaviors and choices.

The specific effects of sexual abuse are as varied as the victims. Much research has been done on the trauma to female victims and it could be assumed that male victims are affected in the same ways. However, there is a substantial difference between the two induced by our cultural expectations of men. In her book, *The Best Kept Secret: Sexual Abuse of Children*, Francis Rush writes:

"In a culture where male sexuality represents strength, superiority, dominance and success, in a world where the desired image is a male image, it is not surprising that a male child will react differently to a sexual experience than a female child" (176).

Some of the misunderstanding about male sexual victimization is due to the silence surrounding it in our society. In his article "Suffering in Silence," M. Nasjlet explains that masculinity is equated with an absence of helplessness, and passivity is equated with homosexuality. These perceptions cause the male victim of sexual abuse to suffer silently. He feels ashamed, fears he is mentally ill, and fears the development of homosexual identification (15). The cultural expectation that men are the sexual aggressors "and they are thought to be weak or foolish if they reveal fear or confusion about sexual functioning" (141) is also discussed by Drs. Diana and Louis Everstine in their book *Sexual Trauma in Children and Adolescents*. They continue saying:

"These factors compound the problem of the molested child because his enticement into premature sexual activity may cast doubt on his fitness for the man's role....It is clear that molestation does more harm than simply arresting a boy's sexual development. It calls into question his fortitude in defending the values he was taught at an early age – in effect, his moral fiber and masculine identity (141)."

Besides arresting a boy's sexual development, victimization may cause him to shut down emotionally. Janet Woititz, in her book *Healing Your Sexual Self*, maintains that the psychic pain of sexual abuse can be so intolerable that the victim literally ceases to feel. The victim will deny that the impact of the sexual abuse was profound and he will react as if he were a casual observer. This emotional shutting down can carry into adulthood becoming an automatic response to stressful situations (24).

In an anonymous interview a victim I spoke with said he had always been very even tempered and showed little emotion until the secrecy surrounding his sexual abuse was broken. It took a long time before he was even able to feel anger against his perpetrator. He had shut down emotionally so completely that it was hard for him to accept the fact that he even had the right to be angry at what had happened to him.

A very important part of healing for the victim of sexual assault is to get in touch with the feelings associated with his victimization. These feelings can be extremely painful and confusing, especially if the perpetrator was someone the victim trusted and admired. In the book *Courage to Heal – A Guide for Women Survivors of Child Sexual Abuse*, Ellen Bass states that the feelings of love and trust are betrayed causing such great pain, rage, and fear that the victim is unable to experience them fully and continue to function (192). Survivors of sexual abuse not only feel betrayed by the person who victimized them, but they also feel that they have betrayed themselves by participating, although they were helpless to prevent it.

It is important that the victim work through his anger and rage. Rarely can this be done alone. The help of a professional counselor or support group is normally required to bring the anger and feelings of victimization to the surface and resolve them. If the victim continues to deny his feelings and is unable to focus his rage at the abuser, it will go somewhere else. Bass states that "many survivors turn in on themselves, leading to depression and self-destruction." She goes on to say that victims may feel themselves essentially bad, criticize themselves relentlessly and devalue themselves. Having blamed themselves, victims stay angry at the child within – the child who was vulnerable and unable to protect himself (123).

Feelings of worthlessness and helplessness form the basis for toxic shame. John Bradshaw, in his book *Healing the Shame That Binds You*, writes that "Sexual abuse is the most shaming of all abuse. It takes less sexual abuse than any other form of abuse to induce shame" (48). Part of the reason for this is because sex is so hidden, so secret. Most people normally feel some degree of shame about sex, but when a young man is molested the shame becomes overwhelming. The victim feels humiliated, degraded, and worthless. He is given the message that he is of little value and has no rights. His boundaries are violated and he is no longer in control of his life.

It is important to understand the difference between shame and guilt. Terry Kellogg, on his video tape "Shame and Recovery," gives this difference: "Shame is about who we are. Guilt is about what we do. Shame is: I am a mistake. Guilt is: I made a mistake." If victims do not tell anyone about the sexual abuse then they internalize the humiliation and become shame-based. When most of our behavior is based on the shameful feelings we have about ourselves, Kellogg maintains we are shame-based. Each survivor of sexual abuse will act out his shame differently, but many men are in prison because they have such a low opinion of themselves that they don't care what they do or what happens to them.

Another aspect of shame is perfectionism. Kellogg states that "A lot of perfectionism is an attempt to repair broken integrity, the broken hurt self." It is difficult for a perfectionist to admit being human. He can act this out by being meticulous with his appearance, being very rigid in his relationships, or being unable to deal with his mistakes.

One major result of shame is lack of intimacy. "It is difficult to let someone get close to you if you feel defective and flawed as a human being" (Bradshaw 25). In addition, the overwhelming betrayal felt by the victim of sexual abuse deeply erodes his ability to trust other people and even to trust himself. Both the toxic shame and inability to trust have dire consequences when the victim is attempting to form intimate relationships. It is particularly difficult in marriage if the victim continues to carry the secret and not reveal it to his spouse. "Many survivors of sexual abuse will not tell their partners because they fear abandonment or an attitude by the partner that they are 'damaged' or were in some way responsible" (Woititz 70).

This continued silence creates the basis for a secret life and the fear that if my spouse knew me as I am, she wouldn't love me. This is especially poignant because of the loss of masculinity the victim feels. Flashbacks of the abuse and feelings of helplessness may haunt the husband causing him to create a fantasy world in which to retreat and affecting his ability to make love freely. All of these factors will make it impossible to achieve both emotional and physical intimacy in the marriage until the secret is broken and healing begins.

When a victim is out of touch with his feelings, when he operates out of shame, and when he has failed to build any real intimate relationships, he then is at prime risk of becoming a sex addict and perpetrator of abuse. Such a victim has locked inside himself a tremendous amount of anger, anger at his perpetrator, anger at parents who have failed to protect him, and anger at a society that has allowed this to happen. This unrecognized anger is what puts him at high risk to victimize others. It becomes a question of power. His own anger at feeling powerless and victimized, by proving his power over others, victimizing them. Longo Freeman substantiates this in his article "The Impact of Sexual Abuse on Males" by saying,

> "The adult offender still harbors the same feelings regarding his abuse that he experienced as a child…victimized offenders still feel a lack of power and control in their lives… the victimized offender misdirects his

anger toward others, often in the form of sexual abuse (413-414)."

Patrick Carnes in his book, *Out of the Shadows,* states that, "The addict who focuses on children usually has suffered some interruption of his own development while growing up. There is a part of the addict which is not any older than the victim" (47). This is especially true of sexual addicts who were themselves victims. They are very likely to molest boys who are chronologically the same age they were when victimized. This is because even though the sexual addict is externally an adult, inside, his emotional development was arrested at the age when he was sexually abused.

When a parent, doctor, clergyman or other significant authority figure molests a child, the child's entire system of right and wrong is upset. The basic groundwork for morality is destroyed for that child. One of the reasons men in prison hate child molesters so vehemently is because many of them have been molested as children. It is very likely that this is what started them down the road of crime.

There is a progression to the damage done when a young boy is sexually victimized. The child thinks of the adult as someone in authority who is powerful and does not make mistakes. When the abuse occurs the victim decides: I must have done something wrong to cause the adult to do this to me. The result is toxic shame, "the core belief that I am basically a bad, unworthy person" (Carnes 86). Unable to deal with all this inner turmoil the child stops feeling emotions. When this carries over into adulthood then the victim is unable to have an intimate relationship based on trust and honesty. These factors, coupled with the fact that adults do not like to feel powerless and they look for ways to feel in control, can cause the victim to perpetuate his own abuse by victimizing another child. The addictive cycle, thus begun, will usually continue until voluntary or involuntary intervention occurs.

Breaking the secrecy around sexual abuse is of the utmost importance. Victims need to vent their feelings and build relationships based on openness and trust. Everstine says that "The child needs to reintegrate his sense of identity and self-worth at the same time that he needs to find a protected niche within his environment" (149).

To facilitate healing, the male victim, the perpetrator, or the sexual addict must avail himself of one or more of the resources designed specifically for this purpose. Healing is more rapid when a trained therapist is consulted along with attendance at a support group or twelve-step program. Parents United is a group of parents of children who have been molested. They provide information and support for each other in addition to meeting with Adults Molested as Children (AMAC). Perpetrators also meet with these groups at various times in addition to having their own meeting. Professionals in the field of child sexual abuse work as facilitators for these support groups.

Victims who find themselves locked in the anguish of sexual addiction can find help and recovery in a twelve-step group such as Sex and Love Addicts Anonymous (SLAA). Here the addict can experience unconditional acceptance and begin the process of healing by admitting that his life is unmanageable. He then learns that a power greater than himself can restore him to sanity. The rigorous honesty required in a twelve-step program provides the foundation to start rebuilding relationships. The addict takes responsibility for his actions and makes amends where possible.

Works Cited

Anonymous. *Personal Interview.* July 1, 1990.

Bass, Ellen, and Laura Davis. *The Courage To Heal – A Guide for Women Survivors of Child Sexual Abuse.* New York: Harper and Row, 1988.

Bradshaw, John. *Healing the Shame That Binds You.* Deerfield Beach, Florida: Health Communications, 1988.

Carnes, Patrick, Ph.D. *Out of the Shadows.* Minnesota: CompCare Publications, 1986.

Everstine, Diana Sullivan, Ph.D. and Louis Everstine, Ph.D., M.P.H. *Sexual Trauma in Children and Adolescents.* New York: Brunner/Mazel Inc., 1989.

Freeman-Longo, R.E. "The Impact of Sexual Abuse on Males." *Child Abuse and Neglect.* 10 (1986). 411-414.

Geiser, R.L. *Hidden Victims: The Sexual Abuse of Children.*
Boston: Beacon, 1979.

Hunter, Mick. *Abused Boys – Healing for the Man Molested as a Child.* Lexington, Mass. Lexington Books, 1990.

Kellogg, Terry. *Shame and Recovery.* Videotape, Dallas: Family Recovery Inc.

Lew, Michael. *Victims No Longer – Men Recovering From Incest and Other Sexual Child Abuse.* New York:

Harper and Roe, 1990.

Nasjleti, M. "Suffering In Silence: The Male Incest Victim." *Child Welfare.* LIX (1980). 269-275.

Rush, Francis. *The Best Kept Secret: Sexual Abuse of Children.* New York: McGraw-Hill, 1980.

Woititz, Jane G. *Healing Your Sexual Self.* Deerfield Beach, Florida: Health Communications, 1989.

Appendix B: Forgiveness Prayer

This prayer is from *Praying for Miracles,* Fr. Robert De-Grandis, SSJ, and is used with Fr. DeGrandis' permission.

Heavenly Father, I ask for the grace to forgive everyone in my life. I know that You will give me strength to forgive and I thank You that You love me more than I love myself and want my happiness more than I desire it for myself.

I forgive MYSELF for all my sins, faults and failings. For all that is truly bad in myself or all that I think is bad, I do forgive myself today.

I truly forgive my Mother for all the times she hurt me. I forgive her for preferring my brothers and sisters, for punishing me, for telling me I was dumb or stupid. I forgive her for any times she told me I was an accident, or not what she expected. For any ways she did not give me a satisfying mother's blessing, I do forgive her today.

I forgive my FATHER for all the times he hurt me. I forgive him for any lack of love, lack of companionship, and any severe punishments. For any ways he did not give me a satisfying father's blessing, I do forgive him today.

I forgive my SPOUSE, IN-LAWS, RELATIVES and FRIENDS. I forgive my NEIGHBORS, my ASSOCIATES, SCHOOLTEACHERS, CLERGY and SERVICE PEOPLE for any negativity and expressions of unlove that harmed me in any way. I release them now, in Jesus' name.

Heavenly Father, I especially pray for the grace of forgiveness for that ONE PERSON IN LIFE WHO HAS HURT ME THE MOST. I ask to forgive anyone who I consider my greatest enemy, the one who is the hardest to forgive, or the one whom I said I would never forgive.

Thank You, Heavenly Father, that I am free of the evil of unforgiveness. Let Your Holy Spirit fill me with light; let every dark area of my mind be enlightened. In Jesus' name. Amen.

"Bless those who persecute you; bless, and do not curse"
(Rom 12:14).

Appendix C: Resources

We have included some resources that might be helpful. For prayer ministry, we suggest that you seek God in the company of those whom you trust most, and who can support you on your path to healing with wisdom, compassion and confidentiality. May God bless you.

Adult Survivors of Child Abuse
PO Box 14477, San Francisco, CA 94114-0038
(415) 928-4576   www.ascasupport.org

Co-dependents of Sex Addicts (COSA)
P.O. Box 14537, Minneapolis, MN 55414
(763) 537-6904   www.cosa-recovery.org

Parents United
615 15th Street, Modesto, CA 95354-2510
(209) 572-3446   www.parentunitedmidlands.org

St. Luke Institute
8901 New Hampshire Avenue, Silver Spring, MD 20903
(301) 445-7970   www.sli.org

St. Luke Institute is a private residential treatment facility for men and women religious, clergy and others involved in church ministry. The program addresses a wide range of psychological and spiritual problems.

Setting Captives Free   www.settingcaptivesfree.org
This is a Christian Web site offering prayer and free studies for all addictions.

Sex Addicts Anonymous (SAA)
P.O. Box 70949, Houston, TX 77270
(800) 477-8191; (713) 869-4902   *www.saa-recovery.org*

Sex and Love Addicts Anonymous (SLAA)
Fellowship-Wide Services
1550 NE Loop 410, Ste 118
San Antonio, TX 78209   *www.slaafws.org*

VictimPower
www.VictimPower.org is a resource for victims and witnesses of crime, enabling them to have protected anonymity over the Internet while they start a two-way communication with law enforcement authorities. It is especially designed and suited for the needs of victims of sexual assault and abuse, and other offenses that are often difficult for victims and witnesses to report.